Twists and Turns in the Hearts, Minds, and Lives of Women

Adventures in Poetry and Prose

Joan Hough Harrington

TWISTS AND TURNS IN THE HEARTS, MINDS, AND LIVES OF WOMEN
ADVENTURES IN POETRY AND PROSE

iUniverse books may be ordered through booksellers or by contacting:

iUniverse
1663 Liberty Drive
Bloomington, IN 47403
www.iuniverse.com
1-800-Authors (1-800-288-4677)

ISBN: 978-1-4917-8037-4 (sc)
ISBN: 978-1-4917-8036-7 (e)

Library of Congress Control Number: 2015917467

Print information available on the last page.

iUniverse rev. date: 10/24/2015

In This Jail of Pages

The spontaneous overflow
of my human heart
is captured here within,
place, draw, or win.
My fantasies, my wishes, my anxieties,
my fears,
all that is real
and much that is imagined
are now imprisoned in this jail of pages,
hopefully to be read by hot-blooded sages,
those who live close to their own human feelings
and guffaw and giggle when they slip on
old banana peelings.

To those lovely women who shared their hearts' stories with me. *You know who you are.*

To my beloved cousin, dear friend, and helpmate, Max Kenneth Huff, whose family changed their spelling of "Hough" to "Huff."

To my precious daughter, Joan Catherine Harrington, and the love of her life, her wonderful spouse, Steven Farr.

To my six adored, now-in-heaven loves—Patrick Herbert Hampton Harrington, Patrick Hough Harrington, Hugh Pat Tomlinson, John Page (Jack) Harrington Jr., Mary Hampton Smith Harrington Rabelais, and Betty Joyce Hough Davis.

Contents

Chapter I

Love Is Wonderful

Poetry

Poetry should only be read
while lying in bed
alone
or
with a friend,
or best,
with a lover.

There is no doubt,
I'll shout it out,
poetry should be read
while
under the
covers.

I have poetry in my soul,
dear heart,
so come over here.
Let the good reading start!

Come Play with Me

There's a child in me
just waiting to be set free
to romp and play with thee.
She's standing here alone now,
waiting to be shown how
you want her.

She's ready to show you
that she's completely delightful
and kind of an eyeful,
soft, gentle, and warm,
bubbly, giggly, overflowing with charm,
ribald, earthy, and bawdy,
risqué, and yes, even naughty,
so,
if you don't prefer
a girl arrogant and haughty,
then
come play with me,
play with me.

For Cori H.

Playmate

I want a playmate;
I want someone
to sit in the sun with,
to pick up seashells
on the beach with,
and to make love
under the moon with.

What I wouldn't do
to spend the best of my life
with someone who
wants a playmate, too.

I don't want him to
make a bunch of promises
he can't keep,
don't want him to
dig holes in the sand
that get too deep.

I just want us to
play awhile, forget
all our worries, and
smile awhile.

Don't want to
think about tomorrows
that may never come
but want to
forget those yesteryears
and all thoughts
cynical and glum.

I wanna find,
I need to find,
I just gotta find …
Have I found
a playmate who can
change my gloomy mind
and lighten my leaden heart?

I need him mighty bad
'cause I must confess
it's very, very sad;
I fear I've forgotten
how to play,
and I'm sure I don't know
what to play
or when to play.

I need, I do,
someone who
can teach me what to do.

The problem is
one who teaches
usually preaches
and seldom can recall
how to play at all.

Dedicated to lonely women with young hearts.

I Dream

I dream of a lover, so hearty, so hale,
so big, so strong, so brave,
and so very male.
He is but a figment of my romantic mind;
such a man I'll never find.

He does not exist; he is not real.
And yet as I lie here, I feel
the hard maleness of him
against my softness
and the warmth that is his life.

I cuddle close to place my fingers
on his skin, and then
I run my fingers along one big arm.
And where's the harm
when he whispers sweet somethings
in my ears and soothes away
all my fears?

My heartbreaks, my loneliness,
my sorrows, my tears
all disappear, driven away
by the fire-hot point of
a dancing tongue
and the tenderness of
a heart forever young.

What delight is mine
when he pulls me over closer still
until the two of us become one
and we know not what shines
upon us, cool moon
or scalding sun.

A warmth spreads across my loins,
as our bodies, once so separate,
now join
and I know joy.

What makes this moment of pure heaven?
Is it girl upon boy? Is it flesh upon flesh?
Or bodies that mesh?
Oh, so good, so good!
But not the sum total of the here and now.

It's how my soul reaches out
and touches, for an instant, his soul,
my heart, for many, many heartbeats,
synchronizes with his heart,
my dreams meld with his dreams,
my kisses and his kisses become
our kisses.

My cares and his cares slip away
into some nebulous never-never lands,
and time stands still,
as paradise is held in our four hands.

Inspired by Caroline Gant.

Somebody

I want to belong
to
somebody.
I want to be possessed
body, mind, and spirit
by
somebody.

I want to know that
somebody
wants
me
and only me.

That somebody doesn't want
me
to share
my warmth,
my smiles,
my body,
my charms
with
any other
somebody.

This Intellect of Mine

Intellect, you're useless,
your voice is stilled,
you've grown stupid!
I say, without compunction,
you doze,
you sleep,
you cease to function,
you end
when passion begins.

Intellect,
no matter how bright the mind,
you grow hazy,
fuzzy, lazy.
Covered by a shroud of mist
is your golden gleam
when passion enters breathlessly
on the human scene.

Intellect,
you make a feeble effort,
now and then,
to throw off the covers of sensation,
to think instead of feel.

But if accomplish this you must,
with one cerebral thrust
you change magic stardust
into sterile soil,
our hours lose all joy,
and time is filled with
tedium and toil.

Platonic

Let's keep it all platonic, man.
I know that if we try, we can, we can,
so don't put your arms around me.
Don't look at me with those great big eyes
that look and see
right into the souls of girls like me.

Don't let your words create a magic all their own
when you talk to me so huskily on the telephone.
Don't stand up so tall.
Don't put your warm, hard body so near me
when you hand me that shawl.

Don't laugh quite so much.
Don't be such a such and such!
Don't share your dreams,
and I won't share mine.
Don't let your eyes get that red-hot shine.

Don't praise my looks.
Don't read my books.
Don't tell me I'm a dynamite girl!
Take care, take care,
'cause dynamite, as everyone knows,
takes everything with it
once it goes.

Don't make me stand on tiptoe and
then kiss my nose.
Let's keep it all platonic, man.
We can, we can. I know we can.
Let's not smile, not laugh,
not touch, not kiss,
at least not much!

Only a little,
like this,
like this.

Enchantment

What have you done to me?
What strange incantations have you used on me?
In a blackened kettle did you toss
the eye of a newt, the toe of a loon.
And did you stroke the silken fur
of your night-black cat?
As of Beelzebub,
you begged me as a boon?

How did you change me
from ordinary girl
to dryad,
willing to dance through
the woods
to the tune of your
Pan's flute, then
transform me quickly to
Naiad
as we approached the water
and you switched from flute
to merman's lute
and Neptune's triad?

How do you make my lips curl upward
after what seems an eternity of downward?
How do you make my eyes shine with new delight,
erasing all tears,
my brain forgetting
the sadness of years?

How do you make my feet barely touch ground,
my heart fly so high
it will never come down?

How do you strip me of civilized clothes
and clad me in passion
that grows and grows?

How do you take my complete self
in your hand
and lead me to lie with you,
covered only by sand?

If it's magic, whether by sorcerer
or loving man,
then darling, oh darling,
make it
over
and over
again and again!

Loon—lunatic or a specific type of bird. (Both definitions are applicable.)

I'm Your Color Book

I'm your color book.
Paint my pages.
Color me romantic.
Color me
in luscious, light-filled colors.

Paint me
in warm body shades
of passionate pink,
sensuous purple,
and amorous red,
for a love that is living
and giving
and wild, sweet nights
in a king-sized
bed.

Paint with every hue,
not excluding
green and blue,
a pot of Amaretto
under a golden
rainbow.

Better than gold
is love, don't
you know?

Paint a love-filled world.
Fill it with silver
kisses
and soft mauve sighs,
chartreuse somethings
and nothings,
and caramel-colored,
honeyed unlies,
lavender thumpings
and bumpings, and
black star-studded skies.

Paint! Paint
lilac, soft little giggles

and magic magenta fireflies.

Now, lover, paint.
Now is the hour.
Only your brush has the color.
Only you have the power.

Dedicated to Elaine Collings, Nancy Rachal, Reba Morrison, Nevelyn Faith, Jasmine Morelock, and all other wonderful lady artists who know just how to inspire their men to paint.

Awakened

She awakened for the first time
in she can't remember when,
wanting,
wanting,
wanting,
wanting a man.

Passion flooded over her
from toes to head,
passion in a body she'd thought
was surely dead.

In the mirror near her bed,
she spied her scarlet face and tousled head.

She smiled in sweet anticipation
of just what might come to pass
if she threw off the shackles
of a dear, departed past
and told a certain man
that she could feel again,
actually had free will again.

No longer weeping child
but grown adult,
what would be the end result
if
she told that certain man.
She didn't think she could,
but
now she knows
she can!

Night Dreams

Night dreams
of you touching me,
of you holding me,
of our bodies entwined
along with our hearts.

Night dreams
of me by your side,
of me cuddled close to you,
me feeling the warmth that is
your life.

Night dreams
and the scents of love,
of your aftershave,
of your skin,
of me on you,
of you on me.

How soon, my love?
How soon will my night dreams
become our reality?

The Heart

My beloved,
I know—oh, God! How I know!
The human heart can grow!
Was it only yesterday that
my heart was a shriveled, leaden thing
filled with dead songs?
So sad, so quiet,
so little, so cold,
so soon grown old?

And now, look at it, listen to it,
feel its thunder.
It grows so large it overflows my breast.
Beneath your hand—your kiss—
it becomes a pulsating wonder!

How wildly it dances, loud as thunder
on noisy, pounding, cloven hooves,
and then tiptoes to you laughingly
through all the nights of our tomorrows,
on soft, little, naked human feet.

So alive, so young, so warm,
it glows with heat,
pulsating with that
ancient,
rhythmic,
carnal,
jungle beat,
so very primitive
and, my darling,
so very sweet.

Whatever happened to that small, shriveled,
cold, shrunken thing?
It has grown into a glowing ember.
Breathed upon by the warm breath of love,
it readies itself to burst into flame,
sweet one, dear one,
when it hears your whispered sound
of my name.

Pink Satin

Well, didja like it?
Was it pink on skin white as milk?
Didja like the pink satin?

Oh, that pink satin!
Was it over skin soft as silk?

Did it make you wanna speak love in Latin?

Do you remember the feel of it?
Was the skin beneath it smooth as satin?
Didja like the thrill of it?

Did it make you wanna speak love in Latin?

Didja hold it close and dance?
Didja learn a brand-new step?
Did it make you want romance?
Didja body get new pep?
Was there velvet skin among the satin?

Did it make you wanna speak love in Latin?

And now that it has begun, how does it end?
Are you now deciding, do you know?
Will you be lover, or will you be friend?
Will you stay, or will you go?

Do you wanna speak love in Latin?

I didn't invent it, for sure,
but I oughta get the patent
on a drug called satin,
for whatever ails you,
it can be the cure.

Once you get addicted to the
heart-mending feel
of pink satin,
you'll whisper and then begin to shout
amor in Latin.

Touch Me

I starve,
not for manna from heaven
but for something more divine,
the sweet and tender touch
of your hand on mine.

I broil,
as if in the desert.
My thirst grows unabated;
it cannot be sated
without that smooth-as-liquid
touch of you.

I cry,
not for what was long ago
and far away
but for what could be
but is not,
at least not yet, not today,
the tear-drying touch of you.

I chafe,
I'm raw, I'm bruised.
I feel so painfully used.
I need,
I need to be comforted and soothed
by the soft-as-velvet
touch of you.

I freeze.
The ice surrounds me.
Near zero is my tissue.
The only issue is
will I ever receive the
warming, life-giving
touch of you?

So help me,
save me, touch me,
and let me
spend the rest of my life
touching you.

Can You Ever?

Can you ever learn to love me
so much
you'll long for,
sing a song for,
right a wrong for
my touch?

Can you ever
learn to love me
in a manner
fierce as thunder,
full of wonder,
glory, and such?

If you can, then
take my hand when.
Don't waste our moments;
they are precious
and few,
and I would spend them,
oh, my dear love,
making true love,
only with you.

Désiderata

(List of Promises)

At this very moment, you fear me.
You fear I will bind you to me with
chains of love,
and I will.

You fear I'll make you want again
all those things you once adored,
and I will!

You fear I'll make you remember
what you've tried a lifetime
to forget,
to want what you've learned to do without,
and I will!

You fear I'll open up the windows
of your mind,
and you'll learn all the stars that shine
are in these eyes of mine,
and I will!

You fear I'll take the blindfold
from your hooded eyes
and make you see
there are no lies,
the sky actually is blue,
my arms do tell you
all that's real and true,
and I will!

You fear
I'll make you love me,
and you'll change
because you do
and because I want you to,
but, most of all,
you fear you'll love me more
than you've ever loved before,
and you will!

Philosophy of Two

Outside,
the snow, the cold,
the night.

Inside,
the warmth, the glow,
the light.

It shines across
the wide expanse
of the king-sized bed
to my side,
touching brightly
my sleepy head.

You hold a book
in your big hand.
You hold my little hand
with your other and
pull me 'round as you read to me
the best that you have found.

I'm so tired, but
I hear the warm, rich sound
of your words,
as the music that is your voice so dear
falls upon my sleepy ear.

Without any further urging,
I cuddle close to your heart's beat.
Your voice becomes part of the
edge of my sleep.

I pillow my cheek
on your hard chest.
What a wonderful place
for it to rest!

What is it that you read to me?
Why, but of course,
it's dear, it's sweet,
it's philosophy.

It's all about life
and loving and caring,
and thinking and giving.

Strange, but can't you see?
You're reading
what we're living.

Together

It's past time, I guess,
to steal a bit of happiness,
so let's!

Let's let our minds bump together,
our hearts thump together.
Let's turn off all the rain
and make the sun shine.

Let's dine on biscuits
and drink wine.
Let's hide from the fierce, cold winter's weather.

Let's throw another log on the fire
and watch the flames go higher and higher.

Let's cook together,
read a book together,
cross a frozen brook together.
Let's crawl beneath some king- or queen-sized covers
like delighted, new yet old, experienced lovers.

Let's convince each, the other,
there has never been another
with whom we have been
together.

Let's kiss and kiss and kiss.
Let's grab, let's cherish
all the happiness and all the bliss
we can't miss,
together!

My Tears Have Gone Traveling

I woke up this morning
with a smile
on my face.
All those tears
have gone traveling
to some other crazy place.

They've left
a certain softness
about me
that wasn't here before.
Guess it must have been hiding
behind the bedroom door.
We only found it
when you told me,
"You, I adore!"

I've changed;
there's a gaiety now
in my laugh
'cause there's
some in my life.
There's a sparkle in my eye,
a bit of wiggle in my walk,
a lot of giggle in my talk.

Boy! Have I changed!
And to think
I have you to thank
for buying all those tears
a one-way ticket on
a Southwest plane.

Now you and I are
holding hands and dancing
down our Lovers' Lane,
'cause those tears have traveled far,
and they won't be back again.

Close to Me

Close to me,
honey love. Come close to me.
Can't you see I need your arms all around me?
Don't you know how good it is you have found me?

All my life,
it's true, I've spent all my nights
just hoping and dreaming of you appearing.
Now you're here; I feel like standing and cheering.

Want you so,
sugar pie. I want you so.
How glad am I that you feel the same as I.
Should you not, I certainly would have to lie
and say,
"You're not wanted anymore.
I'll find some other arms to wrap around me.
I'll find some other lips as sweet as yours."
Yes, I'll lie.
I'll say to you and to me,
"You are not what I want to have and to hold,
not what I want to love, to hold, and to keep."

This won't be.
Thank heaven that this can't be.
Your love for me is mine forever, so
you'll always be in my heart and close to me.

Cybernetic Flirtation

It was a sensation, our cybernetic flirtation.
I was, just for the fun of things,
seeking ancient blood relations,
no thoughts
of swapping golden rings
or of cybernetic flirtations.

But what was the end result?
Now I'm called "member"
of a strange new cult.

I found myself inducted,
all the rituals conducted,
after a gorgeous man I met
right on Internet.

So now I'm a member of
the Cybernetic Flirts.

How true, how true!
Cybernetic flirts,
get to your PCs and
type 'til it hurts!

Right out of the blue
came acceptance, not rejection,
when a cybernetic connection
connected me to you.
At lightning pace
came love and you,
right through cyberspace.

How true, how true!
Cybernetic flirts,
get to your PCs and
type 'til it hurts!

You made your decision,
with computer-nerd precision,
never knowing whether I
was skinny or fat,
short or tall—
none of this seemed
to matter at all!

You had never seen my face,
when you traveled miles
from your space
to my place.
You knew me only by
unspoken words appearing
on glass.

And yet you declared
via Internet
you'd be my lad
and I, your lass.
Said you'd found my
mind delightfully
delicious and keen,
as projected by my
PC machine.

And now a year has gone past.
You know my looks.
You've read my books.
We think our love will last.
Yes, I took you into my life,
and now, there is no doubt,
you want me for the wife
you can't live without.

I find this more than serendipity.
I hope you don't think me flippity,
when I give a special thanks
to all the powers that be,
when, to them I tell,
"Thank you, God,
Bill Gates,
Ma Bell,
and AOL."

Cybernetic flirts,
get to your PCs
and type 'til it hurts!

Love Song to a Seasoned Sailor

Many love songs have been sung to you before,
it's true.
Your boat has so often left the shore,
there's little new
you haven't done before, seen before,
or heard before.

But I, no seasoned sailor,
have no thick crust of salt.

I shine like the sun after a sudden sea-born shower.
I bloom like an exotic South Sea flower.
I glow with all the gorgeous brightness
of stars in an inky sea of night.

All because we love—
I love, you love, we love.
It can't be wrong, because it feels so right!

I Imagine

I imagine
bright sails
on a boat going out to sea,
her captain, you,
her crew, me!

Then

I begin to float,
feet still upon this
grass-green ground.

I imagine
a "glimmery"
Milky Way,
a gleaming Big Dipper,
viewed with
wide-eyed wonderment
by the crew
who is laughed at
by the skipper.

And suddenly
I begin to hear
the lap, lap, lapping
of waves
upon this
grass-green ground.

I imagine
the sweetness of the silence
that fills our night
when all that's land
is far from sight.

I imagine
the smell of salt,
its taste upon
our meeting lips
and
the cooling wake
that splashes us
as we're passed
by bigger ships,

and

I wish,
how I wish,
that we were
out where we
could count the fish,

but

I can but imagine.
It is not to be,
so
I must stand
upon
this ordinary grass-green ground,
and
watch my lover go out to sea.

Rain Song

After the rain,
there's a bit of a
cigarette
in the ashtray by my bed,

and I don't smoke.

There're two
mashed in pillows
by my head,

and I slept on only one.

There's a memory
of snugness, of safety,
of warmth, of tenderness,
of fun,
of great sweetness.

Yes,
the rain time is over and done
but still dancing
'round in my brain.

I'm here now, all alone,
looking out
a very dry
windowpane,

hoping,
hoping,
hoping

for a little more rain!

Intimacy of a Kiss

Ah! The intimate meanings of a kiss,
that peck in the air
near the cheek of a dear friend—
the familiarity of two
who have not seen each other in a while.

That kiss showing one's most intimate nature—
the kiss on a mother's sweet brow.

That kiss between virtual strangers
in an intimate scene of informality but little privacy
in a darkened nightclub.

That kiss conveyed by an x
after a signature in an intimate letter.

But the kiss, revealing to me
the greatest degree of perfect intimacy,
exists only
when your lips meet mine.

It Happened One Sunday Night

A handsome man, attired in black,
placed a big, warm hand on my nude back.
"Turn over, baby," said he.
"I need some loving, yes sirree."
I did, but heck! Gone was he,
only a sweet memory.

If This Is Your Purpose

Was it written in the stars
you'd be sent to me
for me to comfort,
to hold close
in the tender night,
and hear you whisper my name?

Was it written in the stars
for you to set me afire
and warm yourself
in my leaping flame?

Were you sent to me from above
to wrap me in sheets of satin and silk,
to spirit me away on a carpet
woven with threads of gilt?

If this is your purpose
for being, my love,
then so be it, don't tarry,
start being my love.

I am in such a hurry
to throw off this mantle of worry
and get on with the sheer joy
of being your love.

What may have been said to their grooms by the brides of Mike Huff, Dan Smith, and Jim W. Dean.

Dancing on the Patio

The music plays
the melody that is in my heart,
oh, happy daze,
'cause we're no longer apart.

The night is young,
and despite our years,
so are we.
Our song's not sung,
our bell's not rung.
Can't you see?

And so, my love,
our feet still move to the music.
It's true, my love;
if we don't use it, we'll lose it.

The lights are low,
the music is slow and dreamy.
Well, "whatta" you know?
Our wondrous world still grows steamy!

Too old for love?
We say, "But that'll be the day!"
While hearts can beat,
hearts can meet
above dancing feet.

So come, my love.
Put your hand in mine.
Let's dance and make love,
hear the music and sip the wine.

This time is all ours,
our time with the flowers!
We kiss, we melt, we touch—
never, never
too much.

Dedicated to those new lovers who meet later in life.

Reflection

How can it be that when you look at me
I see what I've never seen before?
I see—can that really be
a reflection of me?

There am I, glowing
with happiness,
smiling through tears.
I've never looked so beautiful
as do I when reflected in your eyes.

It is said that the eyes
are the mirrors of the soul.
If this be true,
there is love—pure love, so much love—
embedded in your soul.

I know it's there, I know that's so,
because it adds a golden glow
to what I see—
the reflection of me.

I never knew before
that eyes can look and, in the doing
can melt the coldest heart,
can capture the very essence
of that which is seen.

The warmth in your eyes
is starting tiny fires
in the depths of me.
Soon there will be a conflagration
that cannot defy detection.

I see it all beginning
when I look into your eyes
and see
the reflection of me.

Dedicated to Cherie Davis and her Larry

The Doll

And there I was,
a broken, bedraggled, lonely mess of a miss,
missing way too many of my vital parts,
and then you came.
Looking deep into my eyes,
you saw in me
something worthy of redemption,
so you kissed me,
carefully looked for and
found
all of my missing parts,
and even more carefully
reassembled each little
bit of me
and with your love
made me whole and new again.

Temptation

Temptation!
Oh, the thrill of it.
He smiles, luring you on.
You should have known
he was temptation.

He brings a heat wave
that sears your flesh.
Fire spreads
down to your bones,
impossible to cool.

Now this is temptation.
Your body reacts;
your heart speeds its beat,
your juices flow,
you can't move your feet.

Your lips start to tremble,
your mouth readies to taste,
flutters begin deep within
and don't seem to end.

Enjoy this for now.
Record these symptoms
somehow
so that when you are old,
you'll recall this moment with joy.

It may never happen again,
but if you are lucky,
it will now and then.
Let's hope you'll never, not ever, forget
how a girl reacts to a boy
when there exists
temptation.

An Invitation

You are invited!
Here's your invitation.
I've made us a reservation
for a very special,
very private, very sensual
celebration!

So you choose the date,
and don't you dare be late,
'cause at a quarter 'til eight
dancing will start!

At a quarter 'til nine,
I'll give you my heart!
After a quarter 'til ten,
we'll never part.

Date: your choice
Time: my time is your time.
Place: where the music plays.

RSVP in person.

Bride's Book: A Bride's Words

How sweet it is!
How sweet, the joining
of two hearts, two lives,
two sets of dreams.

How complete it is
when two bodies join
and two souls become one.

How exciting it is
when single minds learn the joy
to be found
in a combination of two.

How wondrous it is
to hold the hand
of my beloved,
to touch the skin
of my cherished one,
to feel my heart beat
in unison with another.

How awesome it is
that a thing called love
makes all this possible.

Dedicated especially to Jena K.

Bride's Book: Heed Not Their Words

Some you know now are
jaded, hardened, cold,
unloving, and unloved.

Heed not their words,
for they never knew or have forgotten
the beauty of shared tenderness.

They know not
the life-fulfilling delight
of shared laughter,
nor the comfort
of shared tears.

They have no magical memories
of nights, of days
spent close while growing together.

Dedicated to Kaylee Kilgo, to Tata Huff, and to the future brides of the Harrington men, Patrick Jordan, Colby Stafford, Mark Allen, Gaelan Scott, and Jonah Blake of Benton, Louisiana.

Bride's Book: Advice to the Bride

Hitch your wagon!
Hitch your wagon to a star.
Fill it with romantic interludes
and quiet times together.

Make room in it,
when the time is right,
for babies and puppies,
and birds that sing,
and families and friends,
and happy other things.

Make time in your days,
always, each for the other.
With fun and simple pleasures,
fill your lives to the brim
and overflowing.

The sweetness you create
in shared moments
will, in time,
live among your greatest
treasures.

Especially for Kaylee Kilgo and the brides of the Harrington men.

A Son's Wedding

There is a time for joy,
and that time is now,
and this joy
will be stored up
among the dearest memories
of life.

I know
beyond a shadow of a doubt
a beloved son
has clasped heart and hand
with the mate chosen for him
by God.

It is this man's destiny.
She will cling to him
through all the days of their lives.
He will hold her close and cherish her
from now through eternity,
for this is the way of love.

And love is the whole reason
for being
and all that gives
our too-short lives
real meaning.

Written to be read by someone at a gathering for a man and his bride.

The Rhythm of Life

Courtships of life have
always been set to music and
the movements of the dance.

Whether to beckon rain
or abundant game,
or fertile fields or fertile mates,
ancients beat their drums,
played their lutes,
blew their flutes,
and became man and wife
while moving in time
with the rhythm of life.

Since this world began,
for every woman, there's been a man,
and together, unless forbidden,
they found a chance
to dance,
especially when the reason
was romance.

When we're dancing in our jeans
and can be seen
shuffling, tapping, romping,
and doing a lot of stomping,
when we kick with our boots
and make a thundering sound,
we may think we're doing the
latest dance craze that's
come around.

But we're only doing
what's been done before,
somewhere back in time
by your ancestors and mine.

So let your eyes caress this partner
with whom you're blessed.
Let our arms and hearts entwine,
for now, in this moment in time,
I'm yours, and you're mine!
Let our feet do the prancing
while our hearts do the dancing.

Magic steps of happiness
will bring to both our lives
a wondrous state of bliss,
as under modern conditions
we carry on ancient traditions
of romancing
through dancing.

New Year, New Love, New Life

And I now begin again, and so do you.
We begin again, my love, and
hasten to cram into what's left of this too-short span of time
all the contentment two hearts can hold
when they join together and become a joyful one.

Perhaps life is sweeter now that we know it lasts
but the blink of an eyelid and then is gone.

But lest we allow a tear to obscure our vision too long,
we must remember that
ever is it possible
for any little blink to become a playful wink,
and there are many ways
for kisses, chuckles, and laughs
to brighten even some very dark days.

Why Do I Love Thee?

Why do I love thee?
The reasons are quite a few.

I love the touch of you,
the taste of you,
the scent of you,
the sound of your voice,
the music of your laughter,
the knowledge you possess,
the warmth of your heart,
the skills you have mastered.

I love the fact that you are such a neat freak.
Your clothes are always wrinkle-free,
your hair is always cut most carefully,
washed daily,
combed properly.
You even eat your food neatly.

What else?
Your kisses are given mighty sweetly.

I love the fact that you love music
and that hearing it makes
both of us happy.
I love your manners;
you treat me not only like I'm a lady,
which I am,
but like I'm precious,
which you make me think I am.

I love your kindness,
revealed not only in your
dealings with me
but with others—men as
well as women,
children as well as grown-ups,
and all of God's critters,
His birds, dogs, and cats.
But let's forget snakes, spiders, and rats
and
never deal with human things like that.

I love your generosity,
your willingness to share
all that you have, all that you are,
all that you can do,
all your knowledge,
all your skills,
and a heart filled with love
for all who love you.

I love your abilities,
most especially certain ones—
those you have and I lack.

I love, love, love
waking up in the morning
knowing you are present
and still in my world,
that you'll phone me
during the day
to check to see if I'm still alive
and let me know you are.

I love it that you age
so beautifully, still look
so handsome—and are
such an incredible,
remarkable man.

I love it that you're honest and honorable,
careful and meticulous,
cheerful and wise.
I thrill at the love I see in your eyes.

Most of all,
I love it that it makes you happy
to love me.

Written in the Genes

The Japanese do it,
the Chinese do it,
the Singhalese do it,
the Sudanese do it,
the Portuguese do it, the Vietnamese do it.
Warriors, the bravest of the brave, do it.

It's done by yellow men, black men,
white men, and red men too.
They all do it; they love to do it.
They live to do it—yes, they do!

It's done by one and all,
the skinny, the fat,
the young, the old,
the short, the tall.

They do it swinging,
swaying, sashaying,
leaping, hopping,
stomping, skipping, sliding, slithering,
squealing, yelling.

Some do it without a sound,
twirling 'round and 'round.
Some in a circle,
some in a square.
Some do it bouncing with wildly waving hair.

Men just love doing it.
Their women do too.
They do it
wearing
veils, hoops, bells,
wedding dresses, G-strings,
many rings, and other things.

Because it's
written in the genes.
Down through the centuries, it's been done
by grown-ups and by teens.
If you don't know that, then
you need to read some!

The birds and the bees do it.
Squirrels in the trees do it.
It's even done by little ole ants!

So let's do it.
Let's dance!

Dedicated to dancers Nancy and Mara and their partners.

Chapter II

Another View

Ambivalence

Forgive me for being this way.
Forgive me
for feeling this way.
I know you can't understand me.
Even I don't understand me.

What's the matter with me?
I'm so confused,
despite the fact
that you love me
and I love you,
or think I do.

Ambivalence is what I feel.
You don't exist,
and yet
you're real.
I want,
and yet I don't.

I can, and yet I can't.
I shall, and yet
I shan't.
Ambivalence!
Kiss me? Yes!
Yet kiss me not.

I run cold.
I run hot.
Turn me off.
Turn me on.
Be with me.
Let me alone.

Love me—no,
leave me.
Cheer me—no,
grieve me.
Hold me tight.
Let me go.

What I want
I don't know.
Will I ever get it
straight?
Will it ever be my fate
to have and to hold?

Do I want silver? No!
I want gold.
No! I want …

Inspired by Caroline Gant

Chopped Chicken Livers

When
one's had
filet mignon,
one
hates to eat
only
chopped chicken livers.

When
one's had
courtbouillon,
it's tough
to dine
only
on
chopped hamburger.

When
one's had
champagne of the finest vintage,
it's
difficult, indeed,
to drink
rotgut liquor,

and

when
one's known
a man
par excellence,
it's
impossible
to adore
un homme ordinaire.

The Mermaid's Lament

Whiskers on his chin,
he's a fisherman
now and then.
He claims to understand
the workings of the fishy mind,
all save mine, save mine.

He lives down by the water
and watches boats
as if by order.
He tells seafood lies
and smiles
in all the mermaid eyes,
save mine, save mine.

His warm heart embraces
the hearts of all fishy races,
all save mine, save mine.

He even kisses with his mouth
every little bass and trout.
He kisses all the faces
and even other places,
all save mine, save mine.

If he chooses to ignore me,
I won't toss my love
into the waves before me
or fling it away to sharks
on some deep-sea line.
No, I'll
save mine, save mine, save mine!

Without You

How I hate to see morning.
How I hate to know that
light will break,
and I'll awake
to another day
without you.

I love the night.
How marvelous when it's time
to turn off the light
and lie down
to a dreamless sleep,
as if I've turned
off my life,
as I would,
as I could,
since it is now
without you.

When I wake up, I know
how little room
I take up.
One girl,
one bed.
How big the bed,
how small the girl,
how large the room
without you.

The sky has lost its black,
has turned to gray.
It's another day!
I cannot bear the thought
that next it'll
turn to blue
without you.

Dedicated to Jo Grey.

On the Value of Writing Romantic Verse

I see you there,
and I know what you're thinking too.
So tell me now,
is this or isn't this true?
You're trying to discover,
do I or do I not
have a lover?

Have I or have I not
known a man,
or perhaps some men?

Your curiosity is such,
you're burning to know
the truth, part or much.
Well, all I choose to say is
what all poets know
the truth is.
One cannot have,
and one can want.
One can cry, but fate can taunt.
One can write
romantic songs or verse
or do what's worse.
One can sit around and curse,
or,
no matter how one once cared,
one can be prepared.

So
now you understand,
if anyone can,
why I write a romantic poem or song.
It's just in case I meet the very right face
to give it to.

If I'm prepared, I can't go wrong
when Mr. Perfect comes along.
So watch while I write
with a hand quite steady.

I aim to be, I gotta be
raring and ready
for Tom, Dick, Harry,
or will it be Freddy?
Or just any guy
who knows how to
wear a tie?

Remembering

It's true you are long gone, my darling,
but still you are here,
held in every crevice deep
in my aching heart.

You have gone far away, my dearest,
but still you are near,
huddled in every wrinkle
in my weary brain.

You no longer hold me, my sweetheart,
but still does your touch linger,
held in every single cell
of my wanting flesh.

Your kisses have vanished, my lover,
but still I know them
as memories on taste buds
in my silent tongue.

The melody of your voice is gone
from my eager ears,
but its echoes do remain
in my heavy head.

Your smiles no longer brighten my world;
long gone is their glow.
Darkness is all that is viewed
by my tear-filled eyes.

Losing you is a most painful thing,
but still I have memories
much too sweet and much too dear,
too wonderful to bid farewell.

I'll cherish them, but as for you,
I'll wash you right out of my hair.
'Twill be easy to do, soon,
when I may
no longer care.

Hey, Fella!

Hey, fella!
Heed these words of fond advice
if ever you value
old shoes and rice
and want your marriage to last.
What I'm gonna tell, and I'll make it fast,
is a secret some guys know, but only a few.
Now one of them will be you.

When you're pledged to a woman,
but you step out of line,
maybe just wink at another female,
just think of this when you look
at that other, pretty young miss.

Most females tell.

What is told, your wife will remember,
'cause you can just bet
women sometimes forgive,
but like elephants, they never forget!

When you've finally found
your true love
whose heart fits yours
like a new glove,
don't you dare put a lingering hand
on some other woman's fingertips,
or your mouth on
strange and waiting lips.

Females tell.

Remember this and remember it well.
Once your own lady knows,
out the window her love goes,
and you're not likely, Mac,
to see it come on back,
'cause you certainly can bet,
she may say she forgives, and yet,

like elephants, women never forget.

A normal female
doesn't want to share her man.
She'll do everything any loving woman can
to hold him to her with chains of love
and help from the
big rule maker above.

The two of you
can dance through life.
She'll be for you a loving and faithful wife,
as long as you
walk the straight and narrow
and always come home
on a path that follows
the way of the arrow.

But should your feet
be led by your wandering eye,
though glib you may be
at selling your wife the big,
the bigger, the biggest lie,

females tell.

Once your wife puts together the pieces,
all real forgiveness ceases.
Do her wrong, she'll leave you.
Do her wrong, she'll grieve you
no matter how much she's been charmed,
and you can't say you
haven't been warned.

She'll tell you
a not-so-fond farewell,
despite her tearful regrets,
because

like an elephant,
a woman never forgets.

Love Letter in the Sand

There it is,
our written-in-the-sand
love letter,
and survive, those words will,
almost as long
as our love.

For we are young
and feel the magic,
the boiling of blood
and the awakening of senses.

And though we are positive ours is true love,
destined for a lifetime, it is not.
Little know we of what changes the years can make
in personalities, in wants, in needs.

Little know we, the important alterations
that will be made,
that as one grows older,
hot fires can grow colder.

You, with more years than I, are handsome, strong, and tall,
so, of course, I look up to you.
With your grown-up height,
you make me feel fragile,
fluttery, and female.
You make my heart sing.

Eventually, as might be expected,
unwillingly, we must part.
I go away to school.
You do not.

I marry another; so do you.
Time goes on and away,
and our mates do too.
But our story is not yet ended.

We meet again at a dance.
Our thoughts run wild
in sweet expectation
and anticipation.
Our eyes meet.
We smile.
We touch.
We dance.

You are a head
shorter than I.

Unspoken

When she was young, she talked.
She, uninhibitedly, told her feelings,
shared her wishes and desires,
verbally acclaimed her loved ones,
shouted her delight,
spoke her appreciation.

Oh my, how she talked.
Often was it said
that ne'r a thought she had
that was left
unspoken.

But now she is grown
and, like the rest of us,
has learned
to hide her dreams,
to hide her love,
to hold all her thoughts close to her heart
and keep all of it
unspoken.

Dedicated to Reba Jean Morrison.

Ode to a Young Man with a Guitar

I see you there.
I'm watching you watch her.
I'm seeing you
come on to her.
Yes, you I do delightedly
observe,
and for you,
here's a wise
and carefully considered word.

Oh! The juices run hot in a young man!
As hot as any juices can!
The juices run hot in
a young man.
He'll steal any good-looking
woman he can!

There you are now
in your early twenties,
growing older by the minutes,
ready for life's new adventures
and the new fall term
with a body quite firm.

Your intellect sparkles
most pleasingly, fellow.
Your voice rings out
melodiously
and mellow.

Your gaze is quite intense,
you fine young prince,
as you glue it to
the lovely, little lady
listening so intently
to the words you sing
and the message
your eyes bring.

Oh! The juices run hot in a young man!
As hot as any juices can!

They cause you to follow her
to the room of rest,
where you hustle right in
and give her a kiss
that's your best.

What a mismatch Mother Nature can make.
Why, she even makes a mountain
where there should be a lake.
But it's with people
she too often screws up,
because she pairs one with another
who is used up.

Those who know their biology know
that what I say is so.
Every forty-year-old female
who is healthy and brave
needs her own
nineteen-year-old love slave.

For the juices run hot in a young man,
hot as any juices can!
Now a forty-year-old woman
is approaching her peak
and needs the very opposite
of weak.

Hers is indeed the need
for a nineteen-year-old lover
on the side.
A man in his twenties
is on the downhill slide.

Oh, the juices run hot
in a young man!
As hot as any juices can!
So, sweetie,
it's sad, but it's true—
that forty-year-old woman
is
too young for you!

Lips That Touch

I see you there—a licking,
a lickin', and a kickin',
a lickin' yo' lips big time.

You see me here, a lickin',
a lickin', and a lickin',
a lickin' lips that are mine

'cause I'm sippin' some very fine wine, but
I ain't sharing my lips,
and I ain't sharing my wine,
'cause lips that touch liquor
will never touch mine!

So stop your wanting and lickin'.
Quit staring and glaring.
Go pester some other
with your tongue and your eyes.
I'll paint you a sign:
only who shells out and buys
can touch mine.

I'm licking my lips 'cause I'm sipping
some very fine wine,
but I ain't sharing my lips,
and I ain't sharing my wine,
'cause lips that touch liquor
will never touch mine.

The Pessimist

A relationship with you?
Well, I'll tell ya
what I'm gonna do.
Forget it!
Simply hold up my chin
and let it all hang out,
with some other guy perhaps,
but not with you.

Why is this?
I think I'd learn to love you so much
I'd become a complete mess.
Mine would be
total unhappiness,
so I'll forget it.
I won't let it
happen to me.

Can't you see?
I've been hurt before,
so I must be careful whom I trust.
I mustn't make the mistake
of thinking love
when there's only lust.

So forget it,
and I won't let it
bring me to the end of time,
with your name written
in some silly rhyme.

Love Letters from Over There

The war meant letters from him.
A heart-shaped chest of them
all wrapped in pretty ribbons
once worn in my hair.

The war meant blue ink
on paper in quickly scribbled
words from him. "I want you.
I need you. I would marry you.
Please wait for me."

The war meant other uniforms,
other outfits, other boys, other men,
and me avoiding too much
closeness with any and all of them.

The war meant love letters filled
with longing from him and from
others begging for my heart,
useless begging. I was too young
to give my heart away.

The war meant young males
returning home,
missing limbs,
missing eyes,
missing lives.

The war meant last letters from
some of them
while they were missing me.

Let My Words Be a Gift to the Wise

When speaking to the lass,
do not praise her eyes of violet hue,
nor her thick golden lashes framing them.

Do not exclaim over her hair
and declare it has captured the sunrise.

Do not sigh over her mouth,
lush and full and sweet that it is.

Do not pant over her body,
curvesome and lithe though it may be.

Do not exclaim o'er her tiny waist,
her slender arms, her lovely neck.

Do not gasp in delight at her shapely legs,
nor at her beautiful breasts.

She had naught to do with
the development or bestowal
upon her of any of the above.
They were but gifts
from her mam, her sire, and her God.

Do, instead, express great delight in
the working of her mind,
for that she herself has hewn
and trained and strained until
it now functions to please her and you.

Chapter III

Inspiration

The Creative

For the creative,
the thing to do is dream.

In their dreams,
their skies are a collage
composed of many shapes
and colors and are seldom merely blue.

In dreams, their thoughts grow wings.
With mouths closed, they sing.
Their brains whirl on a giant carousel.
Their hearts beat as drums,
sans a single sound.

Their eyelids blink,
and the world whirls by shrouded in fears.
Memories are carved
into the growing tree of life
and sprinkled with angels' silver tears.

And then comes the awakening,
and, pen or brush in hand,
pours forth their dreams
in words or pictures
or musical notes captured on paper.

When what they regenerate
pleases them,
that and that alone is their real prize.

But this can only be
for the truly creative—
undoubtedly you and maybe me.

Dedicated to and inspired by my favorite visual artists—Elaine Collings, Reba Jean Morrison, Nancy Angle Rachal, Nevelyn Faith Brown, Jasmine Morelock, and Gaelan Scott Harrington.

Dedicated to my favorite historical poet, Betty Zeitz of Alabama, my favorite lyrical-descriptive poet, Robert E. Taylor, of Australia, and to my four favorite musical artists—Evelyn Clair Hollis Hall, Max Kenneth Huff, Iris Jackson, and George Jackson.

The Kiss

She was so beautiful! Her eyes were sparkling,
her lips incredibly sweet!
It was the first he had ever experienced,
this kiss punctuated by music—
a breathtakingly beautiful melody at that.

As it faded into the night's darkness,
he shook his wife awake.
"Did you hear all of that music?"
"What music?"
she responded.
"The trumpet! Did you hear it?
It was wonderful."

"What trumpet? Oh! Guess I missed it.
Are you dreaming music again?
You'll find your pen and paper there
in the usual place by the bed.
Go ahead! Latch onto those notes
and let me sleep."

And in the course of human events,
he did as he was told.
He captured those notes and
transferred them to paper.

For years afterward,
those very notes echoed through
our days and nights,
filling the airways,
becoming an important part
of the musical heritage of a nation,
all because
some muse kissed a guy.

When "The Kiss" first appeared on a poetry Internet site, a message was received from a musician very anxious to learn the name of the composer of the music. The reader had taken the poem to be a truthful account of a famous musician's life experience. What a compliment for this poet!

I Feel a Poem Coming On

I feel a poem coming on!
When the feeling strikes me,
it strikes me!
Wherever I may be,
I am attacked by a most
welcome compulsion
that, when known, fills others with
fascinated revulsion
and horrendous desire to learn
whose behavior precipitates
this abhorrent condition in me.

Ladies insist I identify their guilty chums,
until I say that if I must tell of one,
I must tell of all
from short to tall,
about whose men are in jail
and who put them there and why,
and who told whom the biggest lie,
and whose ordinary thoughts are too ugly to reveal,
and who didn't tell her husband she's off the pill.

I must tell
who's gained the married beau or cast off the secret lover,
whose car will park
within walking distance after dark,
near whose house that is yellow.

Whose woman is bitchin'
'cause her designated fellow is bringing steaks to be cooked
in another woman's kitchen.

Who's hitting, who's splitting,
whose head is lying
on someone else's pillow
in someone else's bed,
and whose hair is dyed red?

Changing names to protect the guilty is expected.
Truthful names must be rejected,
must be substituted with lies
when a poet writes about small-town life,
as it is reflected
in the eyes of women living quietly and respected
under southern skies.

Put Shakespeare in Your Head

There are those who of music say,
"When you leave the theatre or concert hall,
if you can't hum it or whistle it at all,
it's not good."

And there are those who of theatre and the movies say,
"If there's no passion for life,
no amusing or heart-grabbing plot,
no ear-holding dialogue,
no sneeze-stopping action,
no climax, no denouement,
it's not good!"

And there are those who of poetry say,
"When you string words together,
if you hear them,
and they lack rhythm,
if you say them,
and the words don't fall
smoothly and trippingly
off your tongue,
if, as a literate human being,
you read them
and must work, work, work
to capture their meaning,
as poetry,
it's not good!"

"If the words have no power
to evoke emotions, strong or gentle,
to bring forth
a smile, a laugh, a giggle, or a tear,
or provoke contemplation,
as a poem
it's not good!
If it is too abstract,
and does not conjure up
brightly hued images,
it's not good."

"If it's written only to please the
PhD English majors,
it's written to be
buried in dusty tomes,
only to be read by
the few unchallenged
by esoteric text,
it's not good!"

So

write, please, so
those of us in your audience
can read your words
and walk away
whistling, humming, thinking,
laughing, or crying.

Remember, as you lie there
writing in your bed,
hold Shakespeare in your head.
Remember, William wrote
not a word for the intellectually elite
but only for the bawdy masses,
and they were then, and they are now
the ones who really decide
if it was, if it is, or
if
it's not good!

Country Memories

Water!
Well water—
sweet to the buds of
my young tongue.

Butter!
Fresh churned, hanging down,
down past the dipper
in the bucket
in the cold, clear water.

A big farmhouse!
With a big front porch
and a hall called
an old dogtrot.

Tranquility!
Country peace
floating in flowers,
humming bees,
and trees, trees, trees!

Cows and horses out in pastures!
Peering over barbed wire,
looking at bitter weeds
on the other side
and looking at me.

Creeks!
Flowing bubbly, swift,
then smoothly and slowly.
Icy liquid, clear as glass,
polishing pebbles.

Biscuits and dry salt meat!
What a treat—
a picnic for two kids
barefoot and wading,
wading in water that grows colder
and colder as we
wait happily to grow older.

A fragrant orchard!
Trees made for climbing,
green, green apples,
and tummy aches!

Living leaves on the ground!
Little plants saying,
"Come and dig right here!"
Oh, my southern soul,
peanuts are in that hole!

The smoke house!
Redolent with tantalizing
scents of hams, pork, sausage, and beef,
all prepared and placed there
by a grandfather and his sons.

The table!
Very long, lined with many plates
as big men fill their
hungry mouths before
going back to the fields and the plows.

The syrup mill!
Round and round go the mules.
Out pours the sweet and sticky syrup.
If you're good, you can ride
and taste and taste.

Feeling sociable!
Four-hole privy,
see the moon in the door?
Sears Roebuck catalog.
No slick pages, please.

Early wake-up mornings
on the farm,
cock's crow alarm.
Out we go to milk the cows
in the barn.

Hear the songs!
The milkers sing, "Ohdelee, ohdelay!"
The cows let down their milk
when folks sing that way.

Hens roaming free
return to nests to lay their eggs.
Rooster prances on long legs,
convinced he's king
of all he surveys.

A barn's hayloft!
It's the top of the world up here!
Just look at that cloud.
Don't pretend to parachute down.
Umbrellas not allowed.

Potbelly, black cook stove,
a grandmother's magic,
foods that smack of ambrosia
and taste of love.

Fireplace warmth!
The back of you is hot
while the front of you is cold.
To run around naked,
you have to be quick and be bold.

Playing cards, reading books!
Singing songs, shelling peas!
You do all of these
when the rain comes falling down.

Birds everywhere!
Singing in the bushes,
singing in the trees,
sitting on stumps,
twittering by the pumps.

Winter's done!
Summer's come,
and it's after three.
Down to the pond
for a swim!

Burlap bags
and two syrup buckets.
Who can't swim? Not we!
We have water wings.
Can't you see?

The sky!
After the lamps are out,
the sky is aflame with stars.
Eyes bedazzled, children lose their fears
as night's blackness disappears.

Dogtrot is an architectural term referring to a breezeway built through the middle of old southern houses, mostly created during Reconstruction when all Confederates were turned into penniless paupers.

This bit of verse is dedicated to Marshall Vernon Hough of Slidell, Louisiana, to help him remember his Claiborne Parish childhood's days and nights. It is also dedicated to Jerry Beauregard, Joan Somma, Jerrie Yeager, and all folks fortunate enough to have had a family farm or ranch in their history.

The Breeze

Listen.
The breeze is whispering
through the tender new
growing things
in the ground in your own backyard.

And now the wind rises
to whisper high in the tall pines.
It tickles the fluffy tails
of the frisky squirrels
who've left the neighbors' roofs
to chase about on fences
and in trees and among the flowers
swaying on the ground.

The air moves. It rises, it dips,
it cavorts in its invisible dance.
Of course it can't be seen.

No, it can't be seen
by even the best of us,
not even by the most devout of us.
For even the hardened scientific skeptic,
there is no doubt, however.

There comes a pure, religious,
thoroughly uplifting experience
to all who note its presence
and to the many who hear its whispered prayers.

Indeed, the evidence is quite clear.
Even the flowers bow down their pretty heads,
and the bushes all genuflect
when the breeze passes near.

Dedicated to Max Huff.

Journey to the Seventh Star

Ready yourself; we're on our way.
We're going very far.
On this very day,
we're journeying to the seventh star.

We'll laugh as we go to a far better place
where hatred never shows its ugly face,
where sorrow does not abide,
nor do gloom and misery live side by side.

We go where cares never weigh heavy on a human back,
when you smile at someone, he smiles right back,
a place where lives not a single vestige of human fear,
not a reason for the falling of a single human tear.

A place where teeth and bones and heads never ache,
and bones and hearts and heads never break,
where organ problems are all repaired by a music man
who fixes everything better than any MD can.

A perfect land where people know no pain,
no storms, only gently falling rain,
a place where life is without a single mar,
and no sound is ever loud enough to jar.

Never a voice is raised in anger,
never exists a single danger,
never does a person grow lonely,
never does anyone miss a one and only.

Never does senility enter a life,
nor jealousies come between a man and wife.
Never does a baby cry, and
never do lovers lie.

Never is there a love that's lost,
a life wasted,
a sweet not tasted,
a flower killed by frost.

Never is any human enslaved,
never is there a cause for a man to be brave,
but the question does remain,
is what we gain worth what we lose?

Without noise, can there be melody?
Without conflict
can fascination exist,
or will only boredom persist?

It sounds much as if that seventh star
will, in reality, take us way,
way too far
from all that gives life real meaning.

The sorrow that lets us know joy,
tears that give value to laughter,
salt that makes us appreciate sugar,
pepper that balances the salt.

Bitter that enhances the sweet,
hot to contrast with cold,
agony so we may know ecstasy,
slavery so we value freedom.

Without pain,
how can there be pleasure?
Without agony,
how can there be joy?

And is it not obvious? Can you not see?
This kind of loss takes away
all the reasons
for poets to be.

The Man in the Moon

When the darkness of night is spangled
with the glitter of stars,
and the luminance of the moon
veils its bumpy scars,
when the crickets' serenade
drowns out the owl's mournful hoot,
when after the day's melting heat,
the night air cools me
in my birthday suit,
then and only then do I find the time
to look to the sky,
gaze at the moon,
consider all I've done
and what I'll leave when I die.

I'm just a nothing … think I.

And the man in the moon frowns at me.

I look to the sky in its splendor,
and I feel worse.
I ponder the vastness of our universe
and question, *Is a falling star*
a prayer, or is it a curse?

I think of the moon and the stars and me,
and suddenly I know
I am an ant
and of practically no importance
in the grand scheme of things.
Not for me the role of immortal
or an angel with wings.

And the man in the moon looks askance at me.

Not for me, the role of queen bee,
only that of worker ant.
The voice of reality speaks,
and so I know,
but, sadly,
my understanding wasn't always so.

Once I thought the planet Earth
would wobble on its axis
if I didn't strive to hold it there.
In fact, it would cease to rotate
without my ever-watchful care.

Holding earth in its proper place
meant abiding by all the rules
and doing only,
without question,
what was taught by the leaders
in churches and
in schools.

Of course, then I positively knew
all our leaders agreed on
precisely what was right
and precisely what was wrong,
so sang I, along
with most others,
the true national conformist's song.

Silly me!

Hey!
The man in the moon is grinning at me!

Men have walked on the moon,
because others planned
and sent them there.
Maybe these moon men are
the most important of us all.

But then again,
not a single one of them
ever caught a falling star
or put a moonbeam in a jar.

I suspect they are as am I
in the grand scheme of things.
I suspect that with ants, they all sing,
'cause each and every one of them,
leg by leg,
puts on his pants
just like me.

Hey now!
The man in the moon is smiling at me!

And his smile grows wider and wider
as his face goes higher and higher.
He's aware, he knows,
ants are the creator's own critters.
Of course this is so.

Ants have special importance and graces,
no matter the language they speak
or the color their faces.

Wonderful!
The man in the moon is beaming at me!

Old Folks Paean

Lucky, lucky us!
Heaven is in our hands,
and steaks, thanks to Dr. Atkins,
still sizzle in our pans.

As we travel near and travel far,
we see only blue skies
through the windows of our
moving car.

Even with rain, our skies are sunny.
We shove heartbreak aside
and find things
uproariously funny.

We admit we'd rather live than be dead.
We look askance at sad memories,
court happiness instead.
Lucky, lucky us!

We're counting the blessings
still here for us
and blessing the folks
who still cheer for us.

We're thankful
for roofs o'er our heads,
thankful for
those we love in our beds.

We've money to spend
and flowers to tend.
We can eat what we please,
and grateful are we,
we can still bend our knees.

Dedicated to all the couples blessed with togetherness during senior citizenship days.

Renew

Renew—renewal—rebirth—reincarnation,
a chance to do it all again and better,
another wonderful chance!
A chance to be a friend again and show it better.
A chance to love again and to find just the right mate.

A chance to marry again
and experience happiness
even more than before.
A chance to have offspring that
we can help become
healthy and happy adults.

A chance to think again,
more clearly and brilliantly.
A chance to make this world
a better place as we pass through it.

A chance to read again
all we missed
in a lifetime past!
A chance to write again,
to paint again, to build again,
to create again, to accomplish again.

A chance to dream again,
to wish again, to begin again.
A chance to *be* again,
to see again a sky of azure,
a sea of grass,
the silver of an ocean,
and the blue of a newborn's eyes.

A Lovely Lady of Natchez

A lovely lady of Natchez
wears dresses of lavender patches.
Her radiant smile brightens
everyone's day.

She's a veritable Natchez morning sunray
as she pours coffee into cups
and gives morning start-ups
to all who appear unwilling,
unsteady, or just not quite ready
to start a new day's cycle,
folks such as
Elizabeth and Michael.

And never is the lady sweeter
than when she serves
sandwiches for brunch to
Debbie and Peter.

Sometimes the lady wearing hot pink
dazzles like the sun
in a Mississippi autumn sky
as she presents bountiful slices
of excruciatingly delicious
homemade Natchez pie.

Despite being surrounded
by marvelous yumminess
and wonderful crumbliness,
as pride in self she regains,
she, herself, abstains.

She knows she's a survivor and
a winner
so is striving hard to become
a wee bit thinner.

Despite smiling pink lips
and eyes vividly blue,
she hasn't found a male heart
that's valiant and true.

Despite being cuddly and cute,
she hasn't yet found a mate
to suit.
Despite a body, strong, graceful, and agile,
she's vulnerable, lonely,
and fragile.

What her tomorrows may bring,
no one can know for sure,
but it does appear
with her allure,
her life will not be limited
to serving coffee to go
to some other woman's husband
named Joe
or to living alone
without a man to call her own.

No, she'll have a joyful reason
for being.
Some man will come along.
He'll be big, he'll be strong.
He'll love, and he'll take
a spectacular woman, yummier than any pie or cake.

He'll know that in his life
she'll sprinkle fun and add
more sweetness
than found in
any cupcake or honey bun.

Tangier than sweet and sour sauce,
their life together can be,
spicier than Louisiana hot sauce,
filled with loving, wild and free,
the heat of coffee melting the ice of tea.

A lucky guy will possess
no less,
a drink never boring,
a cup overflowing
with much loving
and much adoring.

Looking Back at Christmas

Imagine! Another Christmas is upon us!

It seems only yesterday
I became a wife on a Christmas Eve.
The ceremony was lovely,
the wee church full to overflowing.

And a new husband whispered
that I was the best present
Santa had ever left him
under a Christmas tree.

There after followed years
of putting up little Christmas trees
and buying on-sale toys,
even on Christmas Eve.

There were so many
wonderful Christmas mornings
when colorful paper and ribbons
were strewn all over our house.

There were heavenly smells of Christmas
in a kitchen
and church services
filled with the joyful songs of angels.

At dinner at my parents' home,
there was a gathering of all of us,
grandparents, parents, and children,
and food that only my mother could cook.

And then it ended;
the precious time was over and done.
Children grew up,
families drew apart.

Christmas Eve remained special,
but no more family togetherness—
just my husband, our friends, and me.
Then even that ended.

But other Christmases came along,
ushered in by a new husband,
'til illness came into that picture,
and eight years were spent in bedside vigilance.

Then came that first Christmas
spent entirely alone,
iced in, electricity out,
no food prepared.

Plans for travel cancelled.
But I'm looking back
to many long years ago
and a time of tears.

Holidays for many folks
is a season of sadness;
we feel compelled
to miss times long gone.

We think back to when we were healthy, happy,
full of hope and ambitions,
and surrounded by people
we cared for, who cared for us.

We must take one quick peek
at those laughing faces we love
and will never see again
in this lifetime.

Just one quick look,
for to look longer is to miss,
to hunger for, to want—
all that was but can never be again.

I'll take that longer look when I am old.
I'm only eighty-five now and much too young
to dwell on all that can make
a human heart tremble and break.

Instead, I'll think about
the friends around me.
I'll count the blessings
that surround me.

I'll thank the powers that be
for my present, lovely, marvelous
happiness,
and I'll assure myself,
There's more where this comes from.

Hidden

I lie here
shredded, hidden,
about to die.
Soon, I hope.

Above me,
somewhere over there,
I can still hear the sounds
of heavy equipment
digging, lifting.

Their effort, in vain,
if but to save my life.

I feel pain, overwhelming,
deluging all that is left
of me.

All of my yesterdays
stream before me in my mind's eye,
and now pain passes,
and I know relief, blessed relief.

Then appears, in a wondrous glow,
the smiling faces of those
who have gone before.

There, on the edge
of the darkness, smiling through
their tears, are my sweet ones,
my dear ones,
the ones who know now
I'll await them
on the other side of earth's pain,
in a place of joy.

Relationships

Death appeared on the scene.
Silence filled my days.
The nights were never so still,
never so dark.

The heavens seemed to swell
in increasing vastness.
The land my house sat upon
grew wider
and more distant
from that of my neighbors.

The silence of my empty rooms
left a strange sizzle
in my ears.
I could die here, thought I.

It would be days or weeks or months
before my body would be found.
I could fall and break my bones
and lie still until death closes my eyes.
I'd never be missed.

Rarely did my phone ring.
Only once did someone come to visit.
Only a hermit knew such loneliness.
For him, it was both a desire and a blessing;
for me, a torturous existence.

The TV and radio failed to satisfy
my need for spoken words.
The voices I loved and wanted to hear
were no longer to be heard.

Stilled forever were too many voices,
most of the most important ones.
There was no one to whisper love words,
no one to call my name.

Where were the people I depended on?
Where were the old friends and relations?
Where were those who loved me?
Far, far, too far away—

Some in heaven, some in hell,
some in Nevada, and some elsewhere
while I was in a world foreign to me.
I was where? Mississippi.

What I wouldn't give
to hear just one loving voice.
How could I survive
in such horrendous solitude?

As these thoughts flooded my brain,
slowly I became aware
that in reality I was hearing
a deep, familiar male voice yelling.

"Honey, honey, where are you?
How are you? Are you okay?
Do you love me? I love you.
I want a bath."

And then I knew
I was never alone at all.
I'm not alone, thought I.
I have someone who needs me.
I have someone who wants me.
I have a loving relationship
that, while I wallowed in
despondency,
I forgot.

Heartened, I went into the den
and gave my parrot his bath.

Chapter IV

Slice of Life

Objective Eye

I look at him
with a critical but objective eye,
and I find him—if I'm lying,
I hope to die—
completely, utterly beautiful!

What a wondrous thing he is!
What a gorgeous hunk he is!
So tall, so straight, so strong,
so often right, so seldom wrong.

How I love that fair hair of his,
those shining blue eyes of his,
that firm, good chin of his,
those wonderful shoulders
that only grow broader
as he grows older.

Who wouldn't want to embrace
a body that goes with
such a marvelous face?
And how grand it is
to look at those legs of his.

And look at that!
His stomach isn't poochy;
it's very flat!
See that big chest of his?
Such an expanse it is,
and look at the terrific
way his rear end fills his pants!
And, boy, can he dance!

He is so bright;
his brain puts out a
fantastic light.
I love the way he talks,
I adore the way he walks!

Of course, I'd run
a million miles
for one of his sunny, sweet smiles!
He's my honey!
Wanna kiss his tummy?

I can let you have this fun,
'cause I'm his mommy, he's my son
and only a baby not yet one.

Dedicated to Patrick Hough Harrington (1951–2011). Inspired by Cori Guess Harrington, Elaine Collings, Sheryl Huff Gardner, and all women who love their sons.

The Wedding Picture

They sit there
so very still,
so young,
sweet,
eyes shining with dreams
of all the future
will hold out for them.

She is all of nineteen,
while he is slightly older.
They are wearing
their adult, most solemn faces
on this, their so-far
most solemn occasion.

Neither of them,
at this moment in life,
can even imagine
that theirs will be
a time together
filled, chock-full
of anger, of tears,
of disappointments,
of worries,
of pain.

But they dream,
how they do dream,
that there will be
for the two of them
times of laughter,
times of joy,
times of peace.

They dream that the good times
will carry them through life,
and, if bad times should occur,
theirs will be tempests conquered,
companionship enjoyed,
and serenity coupled with humor.

He dies at age ninety-two.
She, not long after.
They spent their two
lifetimes together,
never alone.

And what do you know?
Despite the vagaries
of human existence,
all their dreams
came true.

And so now they lie,
two hearts, wedded still,
side by side
in an evergreen cemetery
in the land they both loved.
Their children, generations of them,
visit the graves.

As long as the visits continue,
as long as their names are recalled,
so long as their genes
help to create others,
they live on.

They appear
over and over
and over again
in countless pictures
of dreaming brides and grooms.

In loving memory of Thelma Elizabeth Sparkman (1909–1997) and Clinton Emmett Hough (1902–1994), Edna Ross Marshall (1850–1915) and Henry Clay Hough (1844–1913), Louisiana America Almand (1856–1935) and Joseph Warren Adams (1853–1945), Betty Joyce Hough (1936–2015) and Charles Travis Davis (1936–2006).

Tenderness

Tender is a mother's kiss on her baby's little shell-pink ear so dear
and a nibble on that same baby's wee toes.
Tender is a gurgle from a babe
when Daddy plays "I gotcha nose."

Tender is a big sister blowing air
with a mighty drum sound
on her baby sister's tum, tum, tummy so round.

Tender is a cocker spaniel that carefully cleans until it gleams
the face of his little human ward,
the one he's assigned to guard.

Tender is a grandfather playing horsy for a small granddaughter
and reciting, "Ride a little horsy to town!
Ride a little horsy and don't fall down!"
and giving her a piggyback ride down to the candy store and back,
then carrying home a little girl carrying her candy in a great big sack.

Tender is a mother's touch,
a father's hug,
a sister's smile,
and
when time flies by, a lover's kiss.

Whenever I think of tenderness, I think of this.

My Mother's Box of Simplicity Patterns

My mother's box of Simplicity patterns
is all I have left of her.
Inside are fragile, frail, sheer
bits of paper
once used to form wondrous
garments for my
sisters and me.

My mother was gifted.
She could walk by a high-fashion shop,
little heels clicking rapidly
until she reached home
and her Singer sewing machine,
where, without a pattern,
she rapidly produced a dress
identical to the one
she had seen—
gorgeous, silky, long,
and slinky.

But the clothes made
from the Simplicity patterns
were the best, I thought,
because they were like those of
my friends.

Who knows when Simplicty
appeared on the Louisiana scene?
Was it when little Depression daughters
were wearing flour-sack dresses?

As I lovingly touch the old patterns
of the beauty that my mother's
swift needle created,
I see the baby clothes, wedding gowns,
and witch costumes of a later time.
I look upon the residue of that time.

I lift the sheer bits of paper patterns
and shed a tear for what they represent—
the love of my mother,
the hours she spent thinking of her girls
as she plied her needle.

The memory of her night-black hair
and her Singer machine lit by the glow of
a single lamp.

My sisters and I asleep in the darkness—
part of an extravagantly beautiful
yet simple
tapestry of life.

In memory of Thelma May Elizabeth Sparkman Hough (1909–1997), in memory of the mother of Neverly Faith, and all the mothers whose sewing clothed daughters.

My Sister

My sister, my best friend,
how lucky am I
because I know you.
How wonderful it is
that I have you to love.

What is most remarkable,
dear heart, is that I
didn't walk up
to you and choose
you out of hundreds
for a friend.

But, then again,
perhaps I actually did,
despite the fact
that you were born
to my mother
and look a lot like me.

Except prettier, of course,
and smaller and younger and
kinder and funnier and with more
self-discipline, a better housekeeper,
better organized, more patient,
more generous,
able to do things
I know not how to do.

And you are even sweeter and neater.

Heck! The more I describe you,
the more I wonder why in the
world I can care about
someone so much better
in so many ways than I.

Where is that green-eyed
devil, jealousy, so many sisters
know too well?
He definitely doesn't
live anywhere near me,
for I not only love you,
heart of my heart,
but I treasure you
as well.

When you appeared in
my life, you added something
monumental to it—
the knowledge that out there
in the world, there is forever someone
who cares for me.

Wherever you are,
no matter how far apart are we,
your love
shines brightly through
storm, fog, rain, heat, snow,
across the miles,
or across the room,
and wherever I am,
it reaches me.

I know you know
that my love does
the same for you.

But do you know that
I will always hold precious
the memories of every single
laugh we've shared,
every single tear we've shed,
every single hug
we've given one to the other?

I cherish every single cup of
coffee we've looked
at each other over,
every single sip of wine
we've talked over,
every idea we've considered together,
every color, every recipe,
every baby,
every stick of furniture,
every husband,
every job
we've ever discussed.

All the things I would say to you
have been said
by many people, many times before.
I cannot create new words
that other sisters who loved their sisters
have not used before.

All the wonder-filled words revealing sister love
have been repeated o'er and o'er down through
the many centuries of human existence
on this planet Earth.
Everything has been said
that has a single bit of worth.

Forgive me because my language
limitations prohibit me from creating something
completely new,
thus adequately telling you just how much your
emotional support, your encouragement,
your belief in me,
your tolerance, your help
has meant to me and placed into me
much that is the good in me.

Someday when
I say good-bye to the earthly me,
I'll close my eyes for the last time,
thankful that there was a sweet,
dear female human being
who loved me just as I was
and took the time throughout
her life and most of mine
to encourage me to
become even more than I was.

My grateful thanks to you,
dear sister—and my love.
You are beautiful.
You are fabulous.
You are fantastic.
You are fantabulous.

And I am absolutely positive
that, despite what others have said
and will say,
nobody has ever had, or will ever have,
a sister as extraordinary as you!

Happy birthday,
my sister,
my best friend.

Dedicated to Betty Joyce Hough Davis, a southern lady, beautiful in body, mind, and spirit. Dedicated to Cori Guess Harrington and her twin sister Lori Guess Sanderfur and to all women who love their sisters.

Twilight

It's twilight.
Every day begins its end
with twilight.
Why must this be?
Why can't it end
with dawn instead—
and thus not really end
but simply begin again?

And why, if a parting must come,
must it come at twilight,
already the most
mournful time of all,
the time when evening shadows
begin to fall
and shades of the past begin to call.

But farewells know no time
or season,
and they choose me and now
and this time, with unknown reason.
On silent, stealthy,
running feet,
they take from me
the most important
part of me.

I can make no preparation.
I cannot hold my breath.
I cannot hold up arms that shake
or still the quake
of my breaking heart.
I cannot aim my feet;
they meander in a stagger
across a suddenly slanted floor.

I have received the message—
the lover I adore
is no more.

Shadows on the Wall

I see shadows on the wall,
shadows of someone very tall
and someone rather small,
and I'm afraid of what I see—

I fear they're monsters
coming after me.

They are moving all about,
opening their mouths
in a silent shout
and kicking up their heels.

One is shaking his
great shaggy head,
right here by my
little bed.

And I'm getting
very, very scared!

Now I see them hug,
like they're falling in love.
Wish they'd go away
and scare some big ole bug
instead of me.

I'll hide my head so I can't see.
Now my eyes are shut,
and it is really dark,
but I hear a sound coming close.

Should I look? Oh my, no!
I just might see a giant, two-headed ghost.
What's going on?
Something is pulling on my sheet.

Maybe the ghost wants it for his own,
or maybe he's looking
for something to eat,
to gnaw on, like my leg bone.

I cannot lie. I'm what Mama calls terrified.
Golly! I feel something warm
and something wet.
Oops! Now I've done it.

I'm sorry, Mama. I'm sorry, Daddy.
I need someone to come change my sheet.
I feel a puddle down to my feet.

Oh, there you both are!
You're already here.
You came in to give me my good-night kiss.
The shadows were really you!

I wish you had told me so.
Then I wouldn't be in this trouble
'cause there would be no puddle.
You caused it. Don't you know?

The Train

Ah! The clickity clack of the train on the track!
Passing before my young eyes, looming over me,
enormous train,
tall as the cloud-filled blue skies.

The tracks gleam with the light of the sun.
Quick as a zip on a zipper, the train moves
over the bridge, on by the houses,
past me, as I stand on my porch.

From the chimney, the smoke puffs out
in billows of black
as the mighty wheels go
clickity, clickity, clickity clack.

The whistle, how grand it sounds.
I know its rhythm.
I know the engineer.
He is smiling and waving at me.

He, like me, wears a red bandana
'round his neck,
overalls of blue,
and a wonderful railroad hat.

If I'm a very good girl,
he'll stop one day;
he'll pick me up
and take me away.

We'll go to the big round house
where the trains turn slowly about.
Just think of that! I'll get to ride
and make the train go clickity clack!

Dedicated to Engineer Clinton Emmett Hough and all those long-time-back little girls who lived by the tracks because their daddies worked for the railroad. And yes, one day the little girl in the poem did get to ride the big coal-burning locomotive engine right into the round house, and her engine turned around.

Yesterday

Yesterday and all my yesterdays
fade into the mist of time,
all the intenseness of their joy and pain diluted
but still remembered—not erased
by the mundane requirements of today.

It was many yesterdays ago that my daddy held me on his knee,
and my darling uncle balanced me in one hand.
And then came the yesterdays when mud pies were
delightedly made, and,
in despair of ever seeing me clean again,
Mother scrubbed my neck and knees
with good old Dutch Cleanser.

In my yesterdays, there was great comfort
and total acceptance and a pride of being.
There was the never-ending knowledge
that my world was stable and secure.

There were gingerbread men, paper dolls, teacakes,
and a shiny, new, two-wheeled Huffy bike
for Daddy to teach me to ride.

I see him now, my dad, in that long-ago yesterday,
laughing—his white teeth gleaming—his dimple peeking
out at me as he ran by my side and lightly balanced
me on my bike, giving me the courage
to ride forevermore independently, all on my own.

I see my dad in that yesterday summertime,
chasing my mom around in our backyard
as she leapt and screamed and vainly
attempted to shake lose a snake that, somehow,
had become captured as it traveled under her arch
and through her sandal.

My dad! Mother's savior and my own!
And there he is yesterday,
petting the bird dog mama after she produced
thirteen worthy puppies.
I hear him talking to her gently after some of the pups
died and she, herself, replaced them at her nipples
with dognapped kittens.

I see my daddy on the yesterday when
I was fifteen, attempting with
embarrassed sincerity to warn me about
boys and sexuality.

I see him as he completed the unusually beautiful
fish pond and its surrounding bench,
and, sitting together, we admired the giant fish swimming 'round,
their gorgeous tails spread into mighty fans.

I see my dad welcoming friends I brought
home from college, and then
I see him welcome my husband into the
family home for the first time.

Yesterdays later, I see him holding
my daughter in his arms as he walked
with her to the corner store for grandmother-forbidden candy.

I see my father laughing with his five brothers and his papa.
Then, yesterdays after, for the first time ever, I see him cry
as he told his dead papa a final good-bye.

I remember, oh so well, that in all of my yesterdays,
I hugged and kissed my darling daddy when
we met again after a separation,
but I don't recall at all
hearing the words "I love you" spoken by
either of us.

We were caught in the spirit of the times,
so this could not be done.

I do know that my father proved his love for me over
and over and over again through his and my yesterdays.
I grow more and more aware of his love
as each of my todays creeps into yesterdays.

I did not see my dad in his coffin yesterday, because
I had a spouse readying himself for his, but I know
Dad knows that a large piece of my heart
went with him to that place where he will
spend tomorrows.

I pray that you, dear reader, will not
do as I did, but take time over and over
to tell your father of your love, for his todays
will become yesterdays far too soon.

Something Wonderful—A Dad

(Words of Comfort on Losing Your Father)

God knows
where something wonderful is needed,
so He sent someone wonderful
into this world—
to guide you, to guard you,
and to help you be
all that you should be.
He sent something wonderful—
a dad
to love you and for you to love too.

Yes, the other day,
What He sent He took away,
but He left behind all that love
for you to pass on to those
with your dad's genes
in future generations.

And He left behind—you!
You, to share with others
during life's celebrations
memories of your dad.

Your pain will reduce in intensity
and, eventually, will cease.
Your tormented mind
will find true peace,
because your heart knows
this parting is just
for now and that,
it's a "sure 'nuf" fact
you'll meet again,
and that meeting will be
something wonderful.

Dedicated to Elaine Collings, Nancy Hunt, Jerrie Yeager, to the offspring of P. Hough Harrington, and to all who have lost a much-loved father.

A Mother's Angel

Once upon a time, not so long ago,
God sent an envoy to earth
disguised as a wee red babe,
helpless and bawling,
kicking and squalling,
dreaming and screaming.

Not a thing of beauty
at the time, but
hidden beneath her thin,
wrinkled skin was goodness,
kindness, wisdom, and sweetness
so great that all burst forth
and covered the babe
with a luminescence that
warmed even a stranger's cold eye,
causing a nurse to say, "Why, this
little thing will one day become a wonder-filled,
lovely adult butterfly."

Miraculously, this babe grew in beauty
from both without and within,
bringing to her parents and the world about her
her all-giving love.
She came into her life on earth
never knowing her own true worth
but knowing what most wise
men spend years learning,
that a heart unfilled
is a heart forever yearning,
that a life without love
is a life not worth living,

that a life of loving
is a life full of giving.

More and more of what's important
in life, this little angel knew,
as more and more this little angel grew,
and, of course, she became
the sweetest addition to a home
that any two parents ever had known.

She continued to brighten the world
of her mom and her dad.
She continued spreading her goodness
and working to separate the good from the bad.

One night while she was sleeping,
her safe, little room magically
changed into a cozy cocoon.
Light pierced the night's blackness
from God's own silvery moon,
until the sun announced
it was poised on noon.

And with a whirr and a hustle
and a brief little tussle,
out of the little cocoon came a
gorgeous, angelic adult butterfly.
Wearing gossamer,
luminescent wings,
shimmering in rainbow colors,
she flew to her mother.

She resumed the human form
of a beautiful,
wonderful, smiling
God's envoy,
sent to bring the world
a message of love, a message of joy.

She was sent to a mother
to know her own ethereal butterfly child
was now a full-grown butterfly young woman,
all grown and readying herself
for flight from the cocoon of her room
in her parents' home,
to a guy with whom
she'd build a new, cozy cocoon
all their own.

Dedicated to Jacqueline Rome Hamlin, Sheryl Gardner, Melissa Wood, Dorothy Clydeen Ekberg, Nancy Hunt, Cherie Davis, and all mothers who love daughters and daughters who love mothers.

Love at First Sight (for a daughter)

The first moment my eyes met yours,
there was love. Yes, there was love.
It burst into being
so suddenly it took my very breath away.
My heart, figuratively and literally, stood still.

Now don't tell me there is no such
thing as love at first sight.
I looked at you, my love, and you
filled my night with light.
You caused me to know
the kind of love that sets every heart aglow.

How I remember—yes, I remember—
that whole entire breathless night
when first I held you close to my heart.
Well I knew other arms had held you.

Well I knew other hands had touched you.
Well I knew other voices had told you
how very wonderful you are,
but from the moment I saw you,
I knew that you were only mine.

And sure enough, there came that time
when there were
only the two of us to explore
life together,
to sing our own duet of mistakes.

But then to paste ourselves into
bits of a wonder-filled puzzle
and take for our own
a magical life as a pair
of two ever-loving hearts.

Oh, how sweet it is,
the life I've shared with you.
But now there are others who may
love you, differently and perhaps
as much, but never more
than I have done and do.

We were tied together once,
with bonds that will never sever,
whether we live one more second
or die in the next breath.
You are mine forever.
You are mine,
and
I am yours.

I will never forget, my darling one,
all the years we've played and had such fun.
I will always recall, whatever is said
and whatever is done,
that we've had more than our share
of love and laughter and joyful tears.

Because of this,
I'll be ready for whatever comes in the hereafter.
There will be no fears,
because well I know,
when my time with you on this earth is finis,
our hours together will not be over.

We'll meet again in the sweet by-and-by
and share kisses and cookies and hugs,
and laughter and toothpaste,
and all kinds of strange and wondrous things.

As one of our mouths sings, the other will join it.
We'll breathe puppy breath together,
stroke soft little kittens' fur,
admire sleek and swift big horses,
'cause we're birds of a feather.

We'll dine in fine restaurants and sit together
on red sofas made of leather.
We'll find a jillion joys to share
and a billion ways to give each other
more of the same tender, heartwarming,
sweet, and tender care.

Other women have daughters,
other women love their daughters,
but none, say I, more than I love you.

Inspired by Doll Harrington Farr, Jerry Yeager, Nancy Hunt, Dorothy Clydean Daniels Ekberg, Sheryl Huff Gardner, and Melissa Gardner.

Free

My Hough pioneer ancestors crossed the stormy seas
with a man by name of William Penn.
The lightning flashed, the thunder rolled,
they said their prayers, they confessed their sins,
they cleansed their souls.

My ancestors!
Each one, a Quaker, meant every word their lips did speak
as they readied themselves to meet their maker.

As offspring of the Puritan faith,
Quakers sought to be free from
an English king demanding allegiance to his religion,
demanding his songs be the only songs sung,
his prayers the only prayers prayed.

To William Penn and God, my ancestors pledged their sacred honor.
They left their homes in a place called Chester,
in a land persecuting all of Quaker or Catholic faith.
They set their sights on a home in a new land
filled with dangers, different and unimaginable to them.

Their journey ended in a tree-filled world
where they began carving a nation out of a wilderness.
They did not battle the native inhabitants of their new home
but purchased land from them instead.

Sworn to peace, believing all killing of humans to be murder,
they cast out many of their sons
who married females not of the faith
or, while hearing the tolling of the Liberty Bell,
chose to support and fight for a fledgling nation.

The new land made them all welcome.
They prospered, as did their new country.
They were a strong and valiant group
who persevered against floods, fires,
disease, storms, snow, and dangerous creatures,
both man and beast.

They gradually lost most of their children to other religions,
to churches that were Baptist, Methodist,
or Episcopal, or Presbyterian, or Catholic.
But never was a religion forced on any descendant;
always the choice was freely made and freely kept.

The seeds of freedom had been planted
and planted well,
so Houghs who came after the pioneers,
down through the many centuries,
did their utmost to keep themselves
and their nation free.

And now there are many thousands
of Americans
who sprang from that same Hough tree.
They share that same Hough belief
that happiness only can be had
in a land where people, more good than bad,
are brave enough, strong enough, and daring enough
to make themselves, to keep themselves, free.

Dedicated to the English American colonists' descendants named Hough (pronounced Huff) and those who spell their name H-u-f-f; to all Houghs arriving with William Penn and those appearing in the colonies before and after him.

The US Constitution does not permit the central government to force a specific church on the people. From the beginning, however, each separate colony/state had the ability to do so, and this was tolerated in America because folks could always move to a different colony or state. The entire concept of separation of church and state only meant in the beginning and means now that the United States cannot do as did the king of England and force a government-chosen church on citizens. Americans back then and today cannot be forced to be members of any specific church by the United States government. The US government can in no way interfere with the choice of church made by Americans or the practices of that religion unless these practices break other laws (i.e., polygamy is illegal, human sacrifices are not allowed, wives may not be beheaded or stoned, etc.).

Amazing Grace

How odd it all seems now
as I look back,
back in time to our first date,
back to the time
when our romance was
shiny, bright,
before we even
had our very first fight.

You were driving, and you said,
"Pop something in the tape deck."
So I did,
and the pipes began to play.

You turned and gazed
upon my face.
"I love that tune.
I love those words,"
you smilingly said.
"Remember and
have this played for me
when I am dead."

So I did.

When We Were Young

Do you remember,
dear friend of mine,
that time when we were both so young and fair?

When twilight was soft
and the whole world seemed to hold its breath,
waiting for the two of us to grow up and grow bold?

Do you remember how completely,
utterly impatient we were,
two young things
standing there on the threshold of our futures,
wanting to be somewhere else,
doing something else,
fulfilling all our yet undreamed dreams?

We danced about, unknowing of the possibilities
and the probabilities before us,
far beyond our childish thoughts.

Knowing only that we wanted something
but not quite sure what that something was.

Do you remember?
Do you remember how twinkly our stars were?
How gentle the nighttime breeze?
How poignant the music was
that played through our hearts?

Do you remember
how together we reassured, each the other,
as we wondered
about the mysterious changes
in our young bodies?

We knew happiness
because we were not just one alone,
lost and confused by the eddies of life moving about us.

We knew the true love of sisters,
all the sweeter because we
chose each other.

What great delight
we had in sharing secrets,
working and playing together,
dreaming,
admiring boys and wondering
why they were so very different from us.

We had no desire to be like them.
We had no desire to be their equals,
because we knew we were so much better!

How sad it was when
too soon we were parted,
never to have our lives touch again
throughout the span
of the years of our marriages,
of motherhood,
and the growing up
and leaving-home time of our children.

No sharing of grief was ours
when we lost, in one way or another,
so many of those dear to us—
husbands, parents, family, and friends.

But miracles of miracles,
now here we are
in the winter of our lives,
and lo! We have found each other again.

How sweet it is to know that
somewhere on this continent
there still lives a someone who remembers a young me,
as I remember her.

How good it is to remember when
we were two friends,
young and ecstatic about
all the tomorrows yet to be.

And now, dear friend,
we are far apart,
and how I hate to even think it,
but glad it is possible,
we are old.

But never mind that.
When I think of you, you're still
wonderfully funny,
bright, clever, gorgeous,
supple, slender—a bit of fun and fluff!

And I love you now, my sweet friend,
as I did when we were young girls,
in a time that seems as if it were
only yesterday.

Dedicated to Reba Jean Morrison of Louisiana and Colorado and all women who loved their childhood girl buddies.

Just to Say Hello, Friend

I write now just to say hello and ask
how has life treated you since last we talked?
I am guilty of losing touch with you,
although I never wanted to,
never planned it that way.

But life beckoned me,
led me
to travel on a foreign sea,
different from the one
floated on by you.

Events beset me that sapped me
of all energy
and took me on a voyage
through a bit of heaven
and a lot of hell.

The weather was stormy.
Gray and dreary were the skies.
Dark days and darker nights
were filled with agonizing sighs
and culminated in painful, tear-filled good-byes.

But all that, thankfully,
is behind me now
as under blue skies I sail,
and the time is here
for me to say that I have long missed you.

I've missed your sweet face,
your wisdom, your laugh,
your serene beauty, your creativity,
and the light that surrounded you
when you entered a room.

I do hope you're healthy and happy,
as are those you love,
that your life has been filled with
the most wondrous blessings
from the good God above.
Please know that I think of you
in sweet remembrance,
and I appreciate, most gratefully,
all you taught me
and shared with me.

Especially for Nancy Angle Rachal. In memory of Beth Broom, Martha Crow, Irma Stockwell, and Joyce Noles.

A Happy Hello, Big Hug

Time was
when we dug our skinny little toes
into wet sand,
took wee shovels and dug
a little river and
made a few mud pies,
which we pretended to eat.

Then, with sticks,
we drew us big
rooms in the dirt
under the pine trees
and imagined them
our house.

You were the daddy,
and I, the mama,
and my dolls were
our children.

You came home
from a hard day's
work,
hungry
and so happy that
the mud pies were
all ready and good.

And that I was there,
waiting and glad
to see you and give you
a happy hello, big hug.

Years flew by,
and things have
changed.
Now the dolls are those
that belong to
our young daughters.

The mud pies are
those made by them.
Yet you still come home
from a hard day's work,
hungry to find
mud pies, all ready and good.

But now four of us girls
are waiting and glad
to see you,
so very glad
to see you
and give you a happy hello, big hug.

Dedicated to all those women married to childhood sweethearts.

Games of Life

Once in that long-ago time
when we were young,
we amused ourselves with cards.
You were my handsome, dashing, young mate,
and I, your glowing, smooth-skinned, barely pregnant wife.

It was with laughter we whiled away the hours,
playing canasta
and winning, even when we lost
the bets we made, each to the other.

And now, dear heart, that time has passed away,
as have you.
Our grown children are gone,
as are you.

As for me, I sit here all alone, my love,
with wrinkles instead of glow.
My eyes have dimmed,
but, surprisingly, I still see
the cards on the table in front of me,
as I, with your sweet memory hovering over me,
play the game of solitaire.

New Year's Day

Bum bum bum! Here it comes!
Yes, it's here!
Ready or not, it's a new day and a new year.
Bring out the punch.
I have a hunch
that soon friendly folks will be near.

Now is the time to let the good times begin,
so uncork the wine,
drag out the fruit cake and gin, and then
turn on the tree lights for one last go 'round
before you take the now sad thing down.

Now is the time to think of the happiest days of all.
Yes, it's time to laugh and recall,
time to re-love, relive, and remember,
time to let go all of those we would,
but can no longer, hold close.

So let's make a New Year's toast!
Here's to joy and happiness.
May we all be able to let go, forgive, forget,
and let live.

And here's to time!
Time for friends to gather together
and know the joy of good weather
under a gleaming moon and a shining sun,
time to count our blessings one by one.

Here's to that special time we hope yet to have,
time for laughter and fun,
time to light a fire and drink cocoa,
time to stuff our mouths with chips and dips
and speak of chewing gum and ships.

Here's to
this moment, this hour, this day,
this year.
Time to add to our precious collections
of smiles, sweet memories, good cheer.
Time to build up strengths to aid us
in our tomorrows
when we meet face-to-face with sorrows.

Here's to this time right now,
time to take a bow,
time to plant a flower and a tree,
time to watch a bird fly free,
time to paint a picture, write a poem, sing a song,
right a wrong,
time to thank the good God above.

We are blessed; we're still here,
can hold the hand of someone we love.
We have the time to pray
for our future to be filled
with hours and hours of happy contentment,
garnished with love.

The Swing

They were always there,
the two of them,
so pretty, so sweet,
all smiles,
swinging and singing
in the swing
in the front yard,
waiting for Daddy to come home,
vying to be first to spy Daddy's car.

One, his lovely,
his loving, his wife,
the other, his precious,
his perfect, his daughter,
his pride.

The routine was set.
When the weather was good,
they waited all polished and clean,
curled and sweet smelling
in the swing on the front lawn,
ready for his kisses and hugs.

Inside, the supper was on the stove,
good and hot.
The table was set.
The coffee
perked in its pot.

A surprise dessert hid in the fridge.
A surprise puppy wriggled
in a box by his little girl's bed.
Life was good.
It couldn't be better.
The grass was green
and perfectly cut,
the flowers blooming.
God was in his heaven;
all was right in His world.

But then one day
with life at its best,
an 18-wheeler hit a small family car.
A swing stood empty,
moved only by wind.
Forever gone were a wife and a child.
A man's heart and his house
were left lonely,
his food uncooked, his bed left cold.

This could happen again
and happen to you,
so make each moment
a treasure.
Be loving, be kind, be true,
and pray the swing in your yard
will ever be full
of the sweet ones, the dear ones,
the ones you love—
the ones who love you.

Chapter V

The Conflicted

Midnight Man

The wine is chilled.
She's steam-cleaned, perfumed.
Candles flicker, reflected in mirrors.
Music softly fills the air.

She'll close her eyes for just a moment,
and when she opens them,
the Midnight Man will be with her.
He knows the way.

He has a key.
He'll park a block past her.
Neighbors will never know
she dares to make him welcome.

This man of hers,
this Midnight Man,
will be up, up, up and away
before the very break of day.

Will she ever discover
he is merely a midnight lover
who is looking for another thrill, another Jill?
Does she think he'll buy a drink
when he can get one free?

Eccentric Woman

She was very proper, so of course
she never raised her voice,
nor shouted 'til hoarse.
Clad in her business suit,
with her hair arranged just so,
her lipstick—smudge proof,
her perfume—subtle as could be—
it could well be said
she was all an efficient businesswoman could be.

Well, her heels were a trifle high—
more than they should be,
and when she knew walking was necessitated,
she hesitated
and, without a speck of mirth, appeared to consider
her considerable girth and breathed a sigh.

Her nails were a bit too long and her polish too black,
but other than that—

She made an efficacious presentation,
smiling, no hint of reservation,
took the prospective renters
down a walkway through its center.

Then suddenly she began to dance,
whirling, skipping, kicking—
kicks of goal-scoring quality.
Was this business frivolity?

She announced as she did her spin, run, and kick,
"Oh, my God! Now I have to spit!"

The would-be renters knew they had witnessed
a ground-covering dance
and observed a woman in a dancing trance,
but their thoughts took a different spin
when they spied a feline
running 'round a bend.

All they could think of was that
the woman had done her best
to kick a cat.
Only later was it clear, the lady
had tried to avoid, not kill,
despite her fear.

Although she might have felt
that killing was correct and right.
The cat was black as night.

Hedonistic Man

As the final bit of the candle wick
gave its last hurrah,
and the lingering ember of a log
lost its glow in a great oompah,
in a room devoid of light,
through the velvet of the night
came her whispered plea.

"Oh love me, please love me.
Will you love me forever?
I'll love you forever,
forever and a day!"

She knew she could, for that was her way.

"Forever is a very long time,"
was his studied reply.
"I cannot tell a lie.
I don't know if
I can love anyone longer than a day."

He couldn't, for that was his way.

A little of her heart shattered.
Suddenly little else mattered.
A bit of her spirit died,
as through two
kiss-bruised lips she sighed.

"I don't know why I asked this of you.
Your answer, I expected; it's true.
I knew, yes, I knew
you lack the tender emotion
that makes possible the great devotion.

"You'll never know what you're missing
by never loving the person you're kissing,
Somehow I knew you'd care only
the little which is as much as you can,
'cause you're just another
hedonistic man."

With these words, she arose,
gathered up her clothes.
She left him
and went where no one knows.

That she had tarried with him
twenty-four hours of a day,
she would never tell,
she would never say.
She would keep her secret well.

She knew she could,
for that was her way.

A Pious Man

A proper and pious man I know
who wears his coat and tie just so.
He is filled with proper righteousness,
and thus,
without his knowledge,
despite the fact he's
been to college,
he sloshes with sanctimoniousness.

In fact, he's instilled with it;
to be sure,
he's filled with it.

Of his morality,
he's exceedingly proud.
Of sex,
he never,
no, not ever,
speaks out loud.

He doesn't drink or dance
or smoke,
would never, ever
tell a dirty joke.

But when the lights
are low,
he's a ready man
who pulls his zipper quicker
than any other can.

This is further proof
of a very ancient truth,
something said best in rhyme.
One doesn't have to
drink, or smoke, or joke
to have a marvelous time.

The Sadist

It's hard to believe,
he's so handsome, so clean,
but
he's a sex fiend.
He's twisted.

Look at his eyes, how they glitter.
It's because his heart is so bitter.
When he sees a pale white throat so fair,
he wants to grab it, then and there,
and choke it
and pull the hair
of its owner.
He's full of such strange hostility,
because
he's twisted.

When a girl turns out the lights,
he grabs and he bites and he bites and he bites.
He squeezes 'til it hurts
any girl he catches who flirts.
He's twisted.

The Problem Solver

I want to solve the problems of all humanity—
the poor, the homeless, the downtrodden masses,
the eccentric, the peculiar, the strange, the paranoid,
the schizophrenic, the depressed.

I would teach them all to look to the sky and fly,
so I'm majoring in sociology and psychology, said she,
speaking to the president of the university.

I'm not afraid to beard you in your den
and make my wishes known.
I'm way too wise to try to
influence you via a stupid telephone.

I know you will oblige most willingly,
once you realize how important
this is to me.

What I want and what I need is
for you, in recognition of my
disability,
to change immediately all my classes to
first floors, please.
That's as high as I can go.
I've acrophobia. Don't you know?

In the Circus Ring

I've come to see the circus.
I hear the band play.
Here's the big tent.
Guess I'll go in.

There's a tiger in the main ring.
There's a circle all of fire,
and the tiger's about to spring.
Up and up he goes
and leaps through burning flame.

And he wears your face,
and he bears your name.

I hear the band play.
Look at the midgets; they're all dressed up.
Here are the clowns too.
One's a tall giraffe
who makes me laugh.
But the silliest one
is you.

And the lions watch your every move.

You flirt with the lady
on the high trapeze.
Her husband's frown,
coming up from the ground,
doesn't bother you at all.
A frown will never make *you* fall.

You kiss her lips
and do some flips
with the greatest of ease.
You're marvelous, you're daring.
You're a clown on a flying trapeze.
Oh, the silliest one
is you.

And the lions watch your every move.

And now you are an elephant
and think yourself so smart
because, as everyone knows,
you can pick peanuts up from the ground
with your very long nose.
Oh, the silliest one is you.

And the lions watch your every move.

And now you're a seal.
You can spin a rubber ball,
and it isn't hard at all.
Yes, you can do most anything
when you're in a circus ring.
Oh, the silliest one is you.

And the lions watch your every move.

You forget that life
is not a circus ring,
so when good men are at home safe in bed,
you do great wrongs instead of right,
and lions don't just sit and watch that sight.

No. *Hungry lions feed that night.*

Obsessive Compulsive

Poor, poor soul.
She cannot walk on a sidewalk
without counting cracks
and counting and counting
and counting.

She cannot lie in bed
without counting ceiling dots
and counting and counting
and counting.

She cannot touch a doorknob
without washing her hands
and washing and washing
and washing.

She cannot go to sleep at night
without checking every door
and checking and checking
and checking.

She cannot leave the house
without double touching
every single cabinet door and double touching
and double touching and double touching.

She cannot sit and rest
without counting and counting
and counting.

Her obsessions are most
compulsive, compulsive, compulsive.

The Mirror

Every mirror would reflect
his golden, gleaming self.
Startling presence was his wealth.
His beauty opened doors
and earned him women by the scores.

Winsome maids pined nightly for his kisses,
so he obliged the silly little misses.

Often he was loved, but never did he love,
but thrilled in taking
and even more in breaking
every single heart
susceptible to his charms.

One young thing, when the affair was o'er,
failed to hurry out his door.
She would not go quietly and leave him alone
but rather did plea and pitifully groan.

He called in a debt owed to him
by a great god above him
and gave the girl a loathsome curse.
Little could be worse.

She must repeat
all that was said to her
and even all
that was read to her.

In lieu of a good-bye kiss,
he renamed the stupid little miss.
That heartless beau
named her Echo.

But with this he insulted one female too many.
Her sisters all joined hands
and beseeched the gods for justice,
and the faux lover fell in love.

What perfect justice! His lover was himself,
reflected in a mirror of water.
His needs were strong, his compulsion so great,
he was forced to kiss himself.

The mirror took away his breath,
gifting him a watery death.
The gods then kindly bequeathed him
a forever look into the water beneath him.

They transformed him into a flower
unworthy of any great acclaim,
admiring itself,
hour after hour after hour.

Narcissus is
his name.

Shadow Dance

I recall
I heard the music. Then
I saw it all.

Through a window,
I saw a woman dancing
in a semi darkened room.

At first I viewed only the shadow
of her lissome form
dancing all alone.

But soon, how evident it was to me
that she was being held close,
her heart as well as her body,
warmed by the memory of some man.

In the background, unobserved by her,
was yet another watcher,
her legal spouse
in his electric wheelchair,
wondering, wondering,
with whom she glided so sensually,
wondering, wondering,
was it he?

Wisdom

Finding the pathway to truth narrow,
lined with the sharpest of knives
and with plants exuding the most noxious of fumes,
we, sensibly, protect our fragile skins
and spare our olfactory senses
by following the wider path that lies
just a bit to the left.

Lined with soft maiden hair
and heaven-scented jasmine,
it surely will take us to the self-same destination,
we, with great wisdom, conclude.

Then later are horrified to discover
ourselves imprisoned somewhere in China.

Dedicated with thanks to those women who bravely walk the knife-lined path: Elaine Collings, Joan Somma, Jerrie Yeager, Caroline Saunders, Judy Menasco, Betty Zeitz, Valorie Protopapas, Carrie Tarranova, Virginia Abernathy, and Clydean Daniels Ekberg.

Chapter VI

Story Poems

Out Walking

Two little kids,
one a he, the other a she.
He's four, she's three.
They're both out walking
when they meet.

"Hi," says she.
"Hi," says he.
"It's my birthday."
"Happy birthday," says she.
"How old are you?"
He says, "I'm four.
I'm bigger than you."

She says, "You're pretty too."
"Boys aren't pretty," says he.
"You don't know that,
betcha, 'cause you're just three.
But you'll get older. Just wait and see."

"Will you marry me then?" says she.
"Heck no," says he. "I don't wanna
marry no girl!
I'm walking."
"I'm walking too," says she.
"Will you hold my hand?"
"Heck no!" says he.

"Happy birthday," says she.
"Now you're eight.
How you gonna celebrate?"
Says he, "I'm going to the rifle range
with Daddy and the boys. We'll have
great fun."

She: "Just make a lot of noise."
He: "Girls don't understand.
I'm walking."
She: "I'm walking too."
He: "And I'm not gonna
hold your stupid hand."

"Another birthday," says she.
"Yeah, I'm fifteen," says he.
"Gonna sneak off to the woods
with the gang
and have a beer bust. Wanna come?"

"I'd better not," says she.
"My folks would
have kittens if they found out."
"Okay," says he,
"then I'll take Betty Jane out and about,
and we'll have a great time.
She ain't so dumb!

"And I betcha I won't ask you again.
I'm walking."
"I'm walking, too," says she,
"and don't ask to hold my hand."

"Give me a happy-birthday kiss," says he.
"Now I'm twenty-four."
"Here's one," says she.
"Tell me if you want more."
"Indeed I will, and yes, I do," says he.

"I want much more,
You betcha!
I want all your kisses,
your love, your hand in marriage,
and all your babies to be mine."

"What!" says she. "Are you crazy?
When in my career I'm doing so fine?
I can't stop now and depend on you.
I'm a liberated woman; that is true."

Says he, "Well then I'll find me a woman
who's ready, willing, and able
to rock my son's cradle.
It's true;
there are plenty of girls who'll do,
and one will wear my wedding band."

"I'm walking," says she.
"I'm walking too," says he.

"But I've changed my mind.
I'll not take no for an answer.
Give me your hand."

She: "Honey, wake up.
The kids have a birthday surprise for you."
He: "At the park again?"
She: "Yes, but at least it's better
than last year's skating rink."
He: "Anything is better than that, I think."

She: "But tonight I have a special gift for you
after the kids are in bed."
He: "They'll go to bed early, I hope."
She: "You betcha!
But for now, get up, start walking, and walk
right over here to me. I love you, baby."

He: "Keep talking. I'm walking.
My! What a busy little hand you have."
She: "Wanna hold my hand? Wanna make me stop?"
He: "No, just keep on keeping on."
She: "You betcha!"

She: "Happy birthday, darling.
The grandkids are waiting to take you
to the park."
He: "They really love to play."
She: "They're not the only ones.
If I know you, you'll want to play
soon as they go home after dark."

He: "You betcha!
Till then, wanna come along and walk with me?"
She: "I'm walking."
He: "I'm walking too, so give me your sweet hand."

She: "Can you believe it, darling?
It's your ninetieth birthday.
Wake up, sweetie. The doctor is on his way."

He: "I've had the most wonderful dream,
We walked down a path by a silver stream,
hand in hand about a mile,
flowers everywhere.
You let go my hand, stopped to pick
a few,
then smiled the sweetest smile.
And you said, 'I'm walking,'
And I said, 'I'm walking too.'"

She: "Hello, Doc. Glad you're here.
He's better.
He's talking, the first time this year.

"Darling, tell him your dream.
It was such a beautiful dream.
Wake up, my love.
Open your eyes, my darling boy.
Today you've given me such joy.
Oh please! Oh my sweetheart!
Oh my honey love!

"I'm sorry, Doctor. I don't think he can.
He's gone walking, and he won't be back again.
But he won't go far; he'll wait for me.
We always go walking hand in hand, you see."

Never Despair

His life—what a joke! What a life!
His wife—what a hag! What a horror!
Nag, nag, nag!
Oh, the sorrow in his every tomorrow!

"Make more money—move your feet!
Get up, get out, get in the money-making race!
Shut your face!"
What a wife, what a life!

"Ask the boss for a raise.
Get out of your daze!
Money, money, money—and some more,
out the door!"
Nag, nag! Vomit in a bag!

"You're a bookkeeper, working hard.
It's been that way for all your days.
Ask the boss.
Get a raise."
Nag, nag, nag!

"You've ruined your eyes,
all for him.
Why aren't you wise?
Get more money! Ask him."

And so I do, and he smiles.
"Bring your wife.
Come to a banquet.
You'll have the time of your life."

"A promotion!" says she.
"You'd get nowhere
if not for me."
Nag, nag, nag!

All dressed up
in bib and tucker,
ready to eat
my banquet supper.
"It's too hot in here,"
my other half claims,
and I'm the one she blames.
Nag, nag, nag!

And now the time has come.
My boss stands up with a smile.
"Vice president," the wife whispers,
and I walk down the aisle.

"Here's your watch," says he.
"The business is grateful.
Yes, indeed, grateful as can be!

"It won't be the same
without your face,
but an adding machine
has taken your place."

Home again, home again.
Jiggity, jig, jig!
A red mouth moves
above a sagging, old chin.

"All your fault! You're a mess!
Oh, I hate you. I loathe you.
I always have, I do confess."
Nag, nag, nag!

And so I sit.
The trial is o'er.
Soon they'll come
and open my door.

I stagger past bars
and sit me down again
and electrically reach
my life's very end.

Wow! Where am I?
What on earth am I to do
in this line at a long counter
with these people of every hue?

"What is this place?" ask I,
when I stand in front
of a long-bearded fiend
and his giant adding machine.
"And who is *she*?"
I ask, pointing to the
counter's very end
where *she* stands.

"Who is that gorgeous,
curvaceous, sweet-faced
young blonde?"
"She's your guide," says he.

"She's waiting to take your hand
and guide you to and through
and stay with you in the
promise land."

"Wow! And double wow!"
says I.
"I've been forgiven!"

"What's her name?"
"Why, what else can it be?"
says he,
and this handsome man grins back at me.

"She's sent to you
by your pope."

I run to her
and hear her say,

"My name is Hope."

"Never Despair" was inspired by a very famous 1923 stage play by Elmer Rice. However, in the poem, the murder victim is different, the finale is different, the perspective is different, and the poet's enhanced idea of forgiveness is different.

A Southern Girl Gone Wrong

But first, background,
before I sing my sad song
about a young, sweet southern girl gone wrong.

She was the mother of two little ones she cherished,
wife of a young marine captain
she'd love 'til she perished.

Born with jasmine and magnolias in her hair
and eight or so uncles, a daddy and grandfathers
to give her care.

She grew up petted and protected,
her independent spirit never developed or respected.
Males were created to do for her, she expected,
and they did.

Although her spouse adored her, he treated her like a kid.
She was, in his view, too kind, too pretty, too sweet
to ever occupy a driver's seat.

At the birthday party, the music played.
Couples whirled about the floor and sashayed.
Her marine bartended for a long time,
so she joined her girl buddies in crime.

Too poor with words to earn acclaim as a joker,
in the ladies' room she became a secret smoker.
The band played, "Goodnight, Irene,"
and the leader told the CO,
"Good night, Gyrene."

All departed to their cars
and drove away under the stars.
Miles down the moonlit road,
their car the captain slowed.

Appearing as sober as the proverbial judge,
one hand on the steering wheel,
he gave his wife a nudge.
"You've had too much to drink, haven't you?"

Deeply offended was she that he could say a thing so untrue.
The only words she would say were,
"Of course not. I only went to the bathroom
so frequently to use the pot."

His accusations and her denials
filled the night,
as with words they chose to fight.
Then just as he had contrived it,
he pointed to the steering wheel and said, "Sober? Prove it. Drive it."

Horror filled her brain.
Her beloved protector had surely
gone insane!
Or worse than this, he must hate her.
He probably regretted he ever did date her.

Declaring war, he stopped the car
and strode to the passenger's side.
The darkness obscured her smile
as she drove out of his sight.

She drove down the road a mile
'til tears flooded her smile,
and back she drove to the place
where she had left his precious face.

He was nowhere to be seen!
Not in sight was a uniform of green.
Where was her lover—her mate?
Had her children's father met a cruel, cruel fate?

She left and returned to the start
where foolishly she had misplaced her heart.
Finally giving up the search,
she surrendered and left her darling in the lurch.

She drove tear-blurred miles to a house dark and eerie
and lay down her head, now grown so weary.
Dawn broke. She awoke
and drove to fetch the children from grandparents' home.

Returned—so sorry, so sad, no ring on the phone.
Car parked, kids in the house,
Mama is the world's greatest louse.
Breakfast done. No fun, no fun!
Out to the car to check it again.
Oops! What's this? Children from church peeking in.
What are they looking at? What do they see?
Ah, they see what I see—
a big, muddy marine looking at them and looking at me!

He's muddy from stern to stem.
Oh, Lordy! But I've done wrong to him!
Will I be murdered right here on the spot?
Never have I been in a spot so hot.
What in the world can I say to make his anger go away?

She pasted on her sweetest smile and said,
"The food is ready, honey.
Come in and eat.
Then you can bathe. Then you can sleep."

He smiled back like a young, sweet thing,
and her wicked heart began to sing.
He climbed slowly and stiffly, as if up from deep pits,
and soon was devouring eggs, sausage, and grits.

Years went by—but not a word of this happening did he mention
'til twas time to draw his pension.
Then, laughingly he spoke
of what he'd decided was the world's funniest joke.

Out there in the Louisiana woods,
he'd tried to climb over a halted train,
when up started the engine
and off chugged the train.

With a very fast, clickity, clickity clack,
he rode from Louisiana to Texas and right back.
He started to climb off, but then
the train backed back to Texas again.

Time passed. The train to Louisiana returned.
Off he got, right back where he'd climbed on.
He trudged through cow pastures
and hiked down country lanes.

He splashed through mud puddles,
was soaked by blinding rain.
By this time, his mind out of muddles,
he felt completely sane.
Reaching home, doorbell unheard, he decided it best
to get in the car and take a short rest.
While dreaming dreams of Natchitoches meat pies,
he was awakened by giggles
and found himself stared at by six pairs of young Christian eyes.

After twenty-six years of marriage, their last four years a honeymoon,
with the final words of his life, he told not a lie
when, with her kiss on his lips, he ran out to die.

He said, "I love you, honey, always
and forever, and you know it, though maybe, always, I don't show it.
You're the anchor that has kept me
from floating eternally on a turbulent sea."

She wore her sweetest smile again when she said,
"Finish your run and hurry home, honey.
The food'll be ready. You can eat,
you can bathe, we can sleep."

"Just seal that promise with a kiss," he said.
She did, never thinking
the next time she kissed him
he'd be dead.

He ran off; he left her.
Neither she nor he did a thing that was wrong.
He had no choice; he had to race to heaven
'cause he'd heard that starting gong.

Dedicated to all wives who love their marine spouses.

Mischief on All Saints' Night

She was in the tub, washing her long black hair.
She heard the ring of the phone.
Where was he? Why didn't he answer? *Doesn't he care?*

It might be the children, thought she.
Wrapped in toweling, with dripping steps,
she hastened to the hall and the phone.

"Wrong number!" she groaned.
"But guess the kids are still happy,
spending the night with friends of their own."

Back to the room of the bath,
but wait! In the mirror! What a strange and funny sight!
Yet on this night of nights, the sight suddenly seemed perfectly right!

She never knew hair could stand up so pointy and be so tall!
Look, it doesn't even try to fall!
Soap does wondrous things!

It can change something beautiful into something weird!
Why, it could even make, maybe,
a wee, little female feared!

Hmmmm! Ideas swirled around in her brain!
She couldn't stop them;
Madame Mischief was back again!

Out to the hall she scampered,
removing a military raincoat (her spouse's)
and a Halloween mask (her kid's) from pegs.
She donned both and glided outside, bare feet, bare legs, and bare under the raincoat, girl!

She laughed her way through a side door and into the front yard.
On the porch of the house,
she heard music from the living room.

Her big, strong, brave, trained-to-kill, marine husband
was in there, listening to his favorite tunes.
Her finger touched the button. The doorbell rang.

He opened the front door and stood there.
In the background, a cowboy sang.
In her best witch's voice, she yelled, "Trick or treat!"

She hurled open the raincoat and bared her bareness,
her bare this and bare feet.
Maybe he thinks about saints. He faints.

About a Real Girl We'll Call Sue

All I tell is true.
Strange, it's so strange. It's hard to believe.
It's a story about a girl we'll call Sue.

Married, sleeping in the bed with her husband
365 nights times six,
her life was in a terrible fix.

It seems all they did was sleep.
Less than five times was she held even sort of close to him,
despite all the tears she did weep.

When her physician examined her condition,
that her life was spent in chastity,
he knew without her husband's admission.

Said the MD, "Truth you cannot hide.
Despite making a baby, because of a section birth,
you are, technically, still a virgin bride.

"Because of the failures of a legal spouse
with whom you share a bed and a house,
what is intact should not be but is,
though, strangely, you have birthed a child that is his."

In a marriage arranged by rigidly religious parents,
she had been a beautiful, bride, willing and eager,
but her handsome husband's manhood
was simply too downright meager.

What a shame, what a waste, when a lovely, bright,
sweet girl marries in haste, and to her bridal bed
as an innocent goes and remains.
Too embarrassed to tell, for years she stayed the same
as she continued to bear a coward's name.

It's hard to understand in this day and time
how she failed to expect loving as her God-given right
and did not flee a man who pushed her away
in day and in night.

Finally, one morning she awakened,
sick of rejection,
with a body and a soul crying out
for husbandly affection.

Incapable of arousing her husband's need,
she saw ugliness in her marriage,
something rotten that wasn't cotton,
and it wasn't she.

Oh, dear, she cried.
Oh dear. What can the matter be?
Moving past embarrassment and emotional pain,
she saw the doctor once again.

Then, convinced and armed with written evidence,
she challenged the man who could not do
what any normal husband would do.

She faced the man ruining her life
by taking her, a naïve girl, as his lawfully wedded wife.
He had stolen from her years of sharing and living,
cheated her of the joy of loving, receiving, and giving.

By his cowardly refusal to come out of the closet,
he broke her pure heart,
filled it with a secret bitter, hidden dark and deep,
guarded to protect a child's dreams and sleep.

Finally, a legal, red-letter day, unchallenged and over,
freed a woman who now can laugh, can love, can play,
can have a wonderful life
with a man who wants a female for a wife.

Chapter VII

Prose

A Teacher from Hell

Third grade—I was not quite seven, a lively, dark-haired, smiling girl. There was, in the same grade, an eight-year-old boy who found my green eyes appealing and my smile contagious. I sat in the front row, almost under the teacher from hell's nose.

She never smiled—she certainly couldn't blame that on us. We were a collection of intellectually superior students, well behaved but eager to explore new ideas.

Because the little boy sat in a back row, he passed the note via the students in front of him to me. I had no idea that the fellow was smitten with me, so I was surprised to see a note. When it reached my hand, I looked down. "Joan, I love you," I read.

Suddenly the teacher from hell grabbed the note, flapping her arms like the wings of an elephant-graveyard vulture. She squawked out a condemnation of my wickedness, unable to halt her flow of venom. How dare I inspire the filthy deed of love-note writing!

In tremulous tones, I futilely attempted to assure her that I had not initiated such correspondence.

Punishment was not to be avoided. The teacher lost all self-control as she screamed out the banishment words sending me into the dark, dank cloakroom.

En route to the dreaded cloakroom and ostracism, I heard the sweet voice of Evelyn Clair, my eight-year-old, best girl friend in the world, lifted in my defense: "Teacher, Joan did nothing bad. She didn't write any notes. It's not her fault that Jack wrote her. She doesn't deserve punishment."

The teacher, infuriated, glared at Evelyn. "I don't care if you are brilliant in math and sing like an angel; you are not an adult. I will not put up with your smart Evelyn mouth! Go join your friend in the cloakroom. You two will stay there throughout this entire day!"

And so we did. I felt sad because I'd been accused of a heinous crime but glad because I had a friend, loyal and true, standing by me.

Evelyn declared, "Right is right, Joan. You're right, she's wrong—even if she's the teacher."

Neither Evelyn nor I, nor any of the other kids in class, ever understood why the teacher became so incensed over a tiny bit of love-letter writing, but most especially why she unloaded her fury on the recipient and not upon the sender.

To this day, I recall nothing that the teacher purportedly presented for us to learn. Strange, but I recall minute details of subjects taught by the teachers who preceded or followed her.

Suppressed, also, are all memories of her scowling face. I do, however, remember her fits and screeches and the overwhelming feelings of misery she inflicted on many of us.

This offers credence to that old saying: *students may not remember subject matter presented by a teacher, but they never forget the feelings the teacher engenders.*

Every Woman's Nightmare

Once upon a time, as a university-level speech teacher, I attempted to encourage my students to lose their fear of speaking before an audience by advising them they should pretend that all in the audience were nude and also to do as William Shakespeare suggested and "screw [their] courage to the sticking point." In addition, I told them they should strive to be so "cool" that even if their own pants fell down, they could, smilingly, pick them up and keep on keeping on—convincing their audience that nothing at all unusual had occurred.

Not very long after, I was in a very crowded Wal-Mart when I heard an unusual popping noise followed by a slithering sound, and I, clad in a dress, felt the elastic in my panties disintegrate and drop the silk things to the floor.

The stuff of every woman's nightmare!

Quickly, I knelt down, placed my purse on my panties, and rose again to keep on keeping on. Shakespeare would have been proud of my courage. The air rising up from the floor was really quite cool, but nevertheless, I think I successfully convinced my audience that nothing unusual had happened—nobody smiled, and nobody laughed!

The Biggest Little Dog in the World

Koora Chan weighed three pounds, but he thought he was as big as his buddy, the big Doberman. He thought he was a strong as his other buddy, the big German shepherd. In fact, he was absolutely positive that he was superior in size to both of these very large dogs.

Of course he was! Didn't he use Si, his German shepherd buddy, as a mattress? Didn't he sleep on Si when the patio floor was cold? Didn't he get to eat the dog food before the big red Doberman named Turk or before Raabe, the young German shepherd, ate a bite? Koora Chan was the king!

Of course, he wasn't treated quite like a king by the white fluff ball known as Quantico, a small bit of a poodle, but what could one expect—she was the queen.

Most of the time, Koora Chan was unaware of the fact that he was a very wee Chihuahua. At times, he even thought himself to be human.

As an almost palm-sized tiny mite of a creature, Koora Chan was brought to live with his people when he was six weeks old. Even then, it was evident that he was brilliant.

There was never a doubt that his was a very high IQ. His attention span was excellent! He listened carefully to each of his human's spoken words and gave every indication of comprehension. His little eyes sparkled as he watched every single move of his humans.

In no time at all, he was following directions and obeying commands, and in no time at all, he had learned to talk.

Strangers came from all about town to hear him talk. Yes, Koora Chan could talk. His vocabulary was limited, but his speech was completely intelligible. As clear as a bell, he could say, "Hello." In fact, he yelled it! He yelled it routinely when any of his people came home. He stood outside on the back patio and belted out his hello word in his very best operatic tones.

All people loved his talking and loved him for doing it, and Koora Chan loved being loved!

When Koora Chan was asked questions requiring a yes or no answer, he always answered with a clearly negative response sound precisely like that of a human, "Uh-uh!" He was often asked, "Koora Chan, are you a bad boy?" Of course he said his no. He was asked, "Is your daddy a good cook?" and he answered with no. "Do you want a whipping?" and his answer was no.

If asked if he wanted to eat, he never said no. And he wouldn't say no when asked if he wanted to go outside. He loved going outside and patrolling the yard. He honestly believed he was keeping away all sorts of cat burglars and bandits—that he was a highly effective guard.

The fact that he was accompanied by his Doberman and German shepherd buddies was insignificant to him when he evaluated the success of each and every patrol mission he undertook. It was always with a great sigh of nighttime contentment that he returned to his spot at the foot of his master and mistress's bed after successfully performing his guard duty.

His hearing was superior, so regularly he would, while still under the bed covers, sound the alarm to announce the arrival of morning and that of a thief (the regular garbage man) stealing the garbage. How dare that man steal the family's garbage! Koora Chan was ever on guard!

Koora Chan had another wonderful ability—one seldom found in members of the dog world. He could stick out his tiny tongue on command. When his mistress told him to do so, when she said, "Koora Chan, stick out your little tongue," he never failed to obey. That was another accomplishment that won him far and wide acclaim.

Often Koora Chan performed for some of his young master's and young mistress's friends. He amazed the kids by proving to them that he was an intellectual snob. He refused to obey any command given to him in ordinary language. He absolutely refused to lie down unless directed to "recline." Without fail, he would refuse to turn around, unless told to "revolve." Hearing that word, he would spin like a top, then lie down and roll over.

When he wasn't sleeping on his German shepherd, he loved sleeping on his master's chest as the master reclined on a couch. Even then, however, Koora Chan was tuned in and turned on to guard and to do so in his most ferocious manner—when anyone dared approach his master or made a menacing gesture toward him.

Family members, awakening before the mistress, were amused to see Koora Chan engrossed in his morning vigil. He stood at the edge of his mistress's pillow and waited silently, motionless as a stone—eyes fixed on her face. When her eyelids popped open, Koora Chan immediately began to wag his wee tail until it seemed likely to fall right off. Never, however, did he give that tail a single wag until she was awake.

Koora Chan brightened the lives of his people for fourteen years before his loving and valiant, wee heart gave out. After his death, he had one more important part to play when in a dream he appeared to comfort his mistress following his master's death. But that's another story.

Love's Healing Dreams: The Death Effect

She was totally and completely wrapped up in her guy. The last four years of their marriage were the best. They had delightful dreams for their future. Alas, all of those dreams crumpled into smithereens while spaghetti was cooking for supper and he, with her kiss on his lips, went outside to run.

After she discovered the only place she didn't cry was in the bathtub, she became the cleanest human being in town. However, the bathtub was not the perfect oasis in the desert of her grief. She continued to feel that somehow, somewhere she had lost part of her body. She stopped locking doors and started hoping the murderer would come in. She had loved her plants—breathed daily on them and for them, coaching them into jungle growth, but she stopped watering them.

The family dogs had received much loving attention from her. Others had to start caring for them.

The wee, old Chihuahua died. He was the smartest dog ever—he could talk. This little dog often had napped on his master's chest.

Losing this little dog was the straw that broke the proverbial camel's back. Her life became completely out of control. She looked outside and saw that the sky was gray, but so were the trees, grass, and flowers, she knew!

Had she gone to a psychiatrist and not told of her loss, she would have been considered severely emotionally disturbed, even mentally ill.

Her mourning had just begun. She went through the entire list of classic stages without knowing they were the classic stages. She knew shock, denial, the making of deals with God if everything could not be a reality, anger at her loved one for leaving her, and finally acceptance of that which could not be changed. She had two amazing dreams, however, which opened the door to recovery for her. Her dreams lifted her from darkness into light.

When her mind knew peace once more, she concluded that one should never underestimate the inner power we each have that can rise up through our agony and heal us. She believed that this power has been placed there by an even greater power and lies dormant, just awaiting that time when we will need it most. "God, give me strength, give me relief from this pain," was her plea. She received it. A new beginning began.

Love's Healing Dreams: The Message

A year after the death of her beloved, the wife had two amazing dreams. In the first dream, a little Chihuahua was bravely swimming in a huge river that appeared suddenly in the backyard. He was swimming energetically and swiftly, his tiny legs churning the water into white foam. The river rose higher and higher until, finally, it reached the top of the highest step to the porch.

The wife tearfully observed the wee dog, noting that he carried something in his little mouth—something oblong, white, slim, and trimmed in gold. Without hesitation, the dog brought the object toward the woman. She ran to the edge of the river and scooped up both dog and object. The object was the very small prayer book she had carried at her wedding—one of her fiancé's gifts of love.

Upon awakening, the woman not only recalled her dream but understood its meaning, at least in part—her husband had sent the little dog across the River Styx with a reminder that he loved her even beyond death.

Love's Healing Dreams: The Ultimate Dream

The ultimate healing dream occurred shortly after the anniversary of her husband's sudden death. The woman dreamed that she and her beloved were riding in an automobile up a very steep mountain road. Everything viewed from the car was gray—gray grass, gray trees, and gray sky—drear, dreary gray! He said to her, "Honey, you need to fasten your seatbelt."

She looked at him, snapped in her belt, and responded, "But, darling, you aren't wearing yours."

Smilingly tenderly, he replied, "But, sweetheart, I don't need one now."

Just as these words were said, the car started downhill, and the entire world burst into glorious color. There were flowers glowing everywhere! Through the open window, laughter could be heard filling the air.

Suddenly, before their eyes appeared a beautiful country club with its grounds filled with joyous people, all beautifully attired. And there was his wonderful mother they both adored, clad in the gorgeous dress in which she had been buried—her Easter dress—and wearing a lovely hat and white gloves.

"I've been waiting for you two," she beamed. "I am so happy that you've arrived at last. I have a table reserved for us. The food here is divine. Nobody ever has to diet, and St. Peter is a gourmet chef!"

"Only I will be staying," said her son. "I just brought my darling girl here so she can stop worrying about me and get on with the business of living the good life."

And sure enough, the next morning, armed for the battle of life with this wonderful dream, his widowed wife awakened and discovered that the intense, almost paralyzing pain she had been experiencing was no longer present. It had disappeared! Eventually, as time passed, she smiled again and knew joy again, but she never forgot who was in heaven awaiting her arrival.

Printed in the United States
By Bookmasters